Michael Gläß

Netzwerküberwachung mit Nagios in einem heterogenen
und Serviceleitstelle

GRIN - Verlag für akademische Texte

Der GRIN Verlag mit Sitz in München hat sich seit der Gründung im Jahr 1998 auf die Veröffentlichung akademischer Texte spezialisiert.

Die Verlagswebseite www.grin.com ist für Studenten, Hochschullehrer und andere Akademiker die ideale Plattform, ihre Fachtexte, Studienarbeiten, Abschlussarbeiten oder Dissertationen einem breiten Publikum zu präsentieren.

Michael Gläß

Netzwerküberwachung mit Nagios in einem heterogenen Netzwerk am Beispiel einer Notruf- und Serviceleitstelle

GRIN Verlag

Bibliografische Information der Deutschen Nationalbibliothek: Die Deutsche Bibliothek verzeichnet diese Publikation in der Deutschen Nationalbibliografie; detaillierte bibliografische Daten sind im Internet über http://dnb.d-nb.de/ abrufbar.

1. Auflage 2008
Copyright © 2008 GRIN Verlag
http://www.grin.com/
Druck und Bindung: Books on Demand GmbH, Norderstedt Germany
ISBN 978-3-640-41301-0

FOM - Fachhochschule für Oekonomie & Management

**Berufsbegleitendes Studium zum
Dipl.-Wirtschaftsinformatikers (FH)**

6. Semester

Netzwerküberwachung mit Nagios in einem heterogenen Netzwerk am Beispiel einer Notruf- und Serviceleitstelle

Autor: Michael Gläß

Essen, 29. Juni 2008

Abstract

In dieser Arbeit wird Nagios als Network Monitoring Service eingesetzt. Es werden neben grundsätzlichen Themen der Netzwerküberwachung Besonderheiten einer Notruf- und Serviceleitstelle dargestellt. Die Arbeit orientiert sich an der Praxis und wird ergänzt durch eine Beispielkonfiguration. Zum Abschluß wird ein Ausblick für weitere Konfigurationsmöglichkeiten, wie Hochverfügbarkeit oder grafischen Visualisierung, gegeben.

Inhaltsverzeichnis

Abbildungsverzeichnis

Abkürzungsverzeichnis

Abk	Abkürzung
BMA	Brandmeldeanlage
BMZ	Brandmeldezentrale
BOS	Behörden und Organisationen mit Sicherheitsaufgaben
DNS	Domain Name Service
EMA	Einbruchmeldeanlage
GAA	Geldausgabeautomaten
GLT	Gebäudeleittechnik
GPL	General Public License
HTTP	Hypertext Transport Protocol
ICMP	Internet Control Message Protocol
IP	Internet Protocol
IPv4	Internet Protocol Version 4
IPv6	Internet Protocol Version 6
LAN	Local Area Network
MAN	Metropolitan Area Network
NSL	Notruf- und Serviceleitstelle
NTP	Network Time Protocol
SMTP	Simple Mail Transfer Protocol
SNMP	Simple Network Management Protocol
TCP	Transmission Control Protocol
TLD	Top Level Domain
USV	Unterbrechungsfreie Stromversorgung
VdS	Verband der Sachversicherer
WAN	Wide Area Network

Tabellenverzeichnis

1 Einleitung

Eine Notruf- und Serviceleitstelle (NSL) beschäftigt sich mit Aufgaben der Sicher-
heitsbranche. Der Begriff NSL selbst wird durch den Verband der Sachversicherer (VdS) definiert. Einzelne Kunden werden mit Hilfe von Übertragungstechni-
ken [1] mit der NSL verbunden, sodass bei einer Störung oder einem Ausfall eine
Meldung in der NSL eingeht, die dann von den dortigen Mitarbeitern bearbeitet
wird.

Um die Bearbeitung innerhalb der NSL sicherzustellen ist es erforderlich, die Server und das Netzwerk innerhalb der NSL zu überwachen und zu kontrollieren.
Die Überwachung der einzelnen Server und sonstigen Netzwerkkomponenten
soll auf Grund von entsprechenden Diensten erfolgen.

Bei zunehmender Größe des Rechnerverbundes ist ein Einsatz eines Netzwerk-
managementsystems zur Überwachung unumgänglich. Diese Aufgabe soll Nagios übernehmen. Nagios steht als OpenSource unter der GPL[2]. Die modulare
Aufbauweise und leichte Erweiterung mit Plugins, Skripten oder eigenen Pro-
grammen ist ein Hauptkriterium für die Auswahl von Nagios als Netzwerkmanagementsystem. Die große Community, die Nagios weiterentwickelt und unter-
stützt ist der ausschlaggebende Grund für den Einsatz von Nagios.

In dieser Hausarbeit wird erklärt, wie die Überwachung der Server und des Netz-
werkes der NSL mit Hilfe des Programms Nagios erfüllt wird. Die Daten werden
aufbereitet um eine unabhängige Verfügbarkeitsaussage treffen zu können. Diese
berechnete Verfügbarkeit kann gegenüber dem VdS, den externen und internen
Kunden als Aushängeschild und Vertriebskennziffer genutzt werden. Einzulei-
tende und notwendige Schritte zur Erhöhung der eigenen Verfügbarkeit lassen
sich zusammen mit dem Hersteller der Server fundiert begründet einleiten.

Da in dieser Arbeit einige Aspekte zur Überprüfung mit passenden Quelltext-
auszügen demonstriert werden, gilt es einige Punkte vorher zu definieren. Diese
beziehen sich vornehmlich auf der Art der Formatierung, um den Leser einen

---

[1]Bsp. ISDN
[2]Die General Public License (GPL) definiert die Lizenzbestimmung

direkten optischen Unterschied erkennen zu lassen, um welcher Art von Text es sich handelt.

Im Nachfolgenden eine kurze Konventionsvereinbarung.

- `#>make all` ist ein Hinweis auf einen Befehl auf der Kommandozeile
- */usr/local/bin* zeigt einen Befehl, Datei oder Pfad im Text
- *cfg_dir=/etc/nagios* dient zur Darstellung von Werten in Konfigurationsdateien

Besonders hervorzuhebende Textelemente werden **fett** markiert.

Diese Hausarbeit richtet sich vorwiegend an Personen, welche bereits Hintergrundwissen zur Netzwerktechnik besitzen. Es werden einzelne Protokolle erläutert und auf verschiedene Fachquellen weiter verwiesen, da diese den Umfang der Arbeit bei weitem überschreiten würden. Zum leichteren Verständnis der Arbeit sind Kenntnisse mit Linux als Betriebssystem von Vorteil, werden jedoch nicht vorausgesetzt.

2 Grundlagen

2.1 Notruf- und Serviceleitstelle

Eine Notruf- und Serviceleitstelle ist eine Institution für Sicherheitsdienstleistungen. Der Begriff ist abzugrenzen von Leitstellen der Behörden und Organisationen mit Sicherheitsaufgaben (BOS), wie Feuerwehr und Polizei.

Zu den Aufgaben von Notruf- und Serviceleitstellen gehören u.a. die

- Erfassung von Gefahren- oder Störmeldungen
- Audio- und Videoverifikation im Alarmfall
- Annahme von Aufzugsnotrufen
- Analyse von Anlagenmesswerten
- Steuerung von Anlagen (z.B. Ampelsteuerungen)
- Überwachung von Öffnungs- und Schließzeiten
- Funkortung von Fahrzeugen oder Sachen
- Benachrichtigung öffentlicher Hilfeleister (Feuerwehr, Polizei, Rettungsdienst)
- regelmäßige Prüfung von Übertragungsgeräten und -wegen
- Disposition von Servicemitarbeitern

Als wesentliches Merkmal ist die Verfügbarkeit zu sehen, da eine Leitstelle ihre Aufgaben 24 Stunden am Tag / 365 Tage im Jahr zu erfüllen hat.

Wach- und Sicherheitsunternehmen, welche eine Notruf- und Service-Leitstelle (NSL) betreiben, können durch den Verband der Sachversicherer (VdS) anerkannt werden[3]. Der VdS (ehemals Verband der Schadenverhüter) ist die zentrale Akkreditierungsstelle in dieser Branche.

Abbildung 2.2: Logo VdS[2]

---

[1]Entnommen von http://www.buildingtechnologies.siemens.de
[2]Entnommen von http://vds.de/
[3]Richtlinien zur Anerkennung VdS 2153

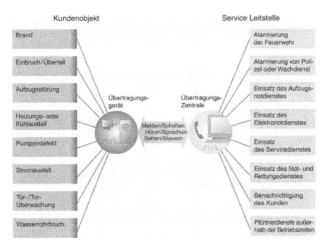

Abbildung 2.1: Dienstleistungen einer Notruf- und Serviceleitstelle[1]

Die Notruf- und Serviceleitstellen werden in folgenden Klassen eingeordnet, wenn bestimmte Voraussetzungen erfüllt sind:

A Empfangseinrichtung für bedarfsgesteuerte Verbindungen

B Empfangseinrichtung für bedarfsgesteuerte Verbindungen redundant

C Empfangseinrichtung mit zusätzlich stehender Verbindung

Die exemplarisch ausgewählte Notruf- und Serviceleitstelle zu dieser Hausarbeit ist Teil eines Verbundes von Leitstellen in Deutschland mit der VdS-Klasse C, deren Abstand als „hoch" eingestuft ist [4].

2.2 Netzwerktopologie

Bei der Überwachung von Netzwerkgeräten ist die Topologie, wie die Infrastruktur aufgebaut ist, bedeutend für die spätere Analyse. In dieser Arbeit wird die Topologie einer bestimmten Notruf- und Serviceleitstelle zugrunde gelegt. Diese Form kann von der in anderen Unternehmen und Behörden abweichen.

Wie in der Abbildung 2.3 zu erkennen, gibt es zwei WAN-Strecken, die zu einer zweiten NSL führen. Es existieren zwei Switch-Ebenen, welche durch Trunks und

---

[4]Vgl. BSI[4], S. 1f
[5]Beispielhafte Darstellung des Autors

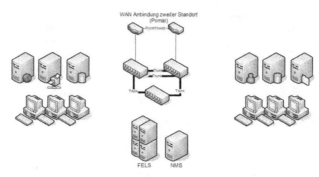

Abbildung 2.3: Aufbau Topologie[5]

aktiviertes Spanning-Tree-Protokoll miteinander verbunden sind. Beide WAN-Strecken sind unter einer virtuellen IP-Adresse zu erreichen. Sollte eine der beiden Strecken ausfallen, so übernimmt automatisch die Andere die virtuelle IP-Adresse. Der weitergehende Netzverkehr wird dadurch ohne große Unterbrechung weitergeführt. Bei einem Totalausfall beider WAN-Strecken werden empfangene Alarm- und sonstige technische Meldungen aus den Empfangssystemen per ISDN direkt an das übergeordnete Managementsystem weitergeleitet.

Gerätname	Kategorie[6]	Beschreibung
SWITCHA	I	Core-Switch
SWITCHB	I	Core-Switch
SWICTHC	I	Core-Switch
WAN01	I	WAN-Anbindung 10MBit/s
WAN02	I	WAN-Anbindung 10MBit/s
FIREWALL01	I	MS ISA Firewall
FIREWALL02	I	IpTables
USV01	I	USV
DNS01	W	DNS-Server
DNS02	W	DNS-Server
WEB01	W	Web-Server
DATA	W	File-Server
AE001	W	Telefonie-Server
AE002	W	Telefonie-Server
DB01	L	Datenbank-Server
DB02	L	Datenbank-Server
TS00	W	Terminal-Server

Tabelle 2.1: Eine Auswahl der zu überwachenden Geräte

Ausschliesslich die in der Tabelle 2.1 aufgeführten Geräte sollen, zur Reduzierung der Komplexität, betrachtet werden. Hierbei gilt es zu berücksichtigen, dass

---

[6]Kategorie I=Infrastruktur, L=Linux und W=Windows

ein Gerät zwangsläufig mit einem Switch verbunden ist. Dies hat zur Folge, dass das angeschlossene Gerät beim Ausfall jenes Switch nicht mehr erreichbar ist[7].

2.3 Dienste

In Hochverfügbarkeitssystemen, wie in einer NSL, reicht es in der Regel nicht aus, nur zu prüfen, ob ein bestimmter Server erreichbar ist. Dies ist dadurch begründet, dass das Betriebssystem des Servers noch auf Anfragen reagieren kann, jedoch die eigentliche Applikation dieses verweigert. Die Applikation, welche ihre Dienste im Netzwerk anderen Computern anbietet, könnte durch einen Programmfehler oder durch Eingreifen beendet worden sein. Ein Test auf Erreichbarkeit des Servers würde so ein positives Ergebnis bringen, jedoch hat dies keine Aussagekraft über die Verfügbarkeit des angebotenen Dienstes.

Nachfolgend einige Erläuterungen der verwendeten Protokolle, welche zur Überprüfung mit Nagios, als Netzwerkmanagementsystem, genutzt werden sollen:

2.3.1 ICMP - Internet Control Message Protocol

ICMP, das Internet Control Message Protocol[8], ist besser bekannt unter der Anwendung PING. Das ICMP dient zur Steuerung und Kontrolle der Netzwerkverbindung. Die Einordnung von ICMP erfolgt in der Netzwerkschicht im OSI-Referenzmodell. Es ist integraler Bestandteil von IP und muss in jedem IP-Modul implementiert sein[9].

Die Anwendung PING nutzt zwei der definierten Pakettypen des ICMP. Diese sind

- Echo Request (Typ 8) und
- Echo Reply (Typ 0).

Die weiteren Pakettypen sollen aus Vereinfachungsgründen nicht weiter erläutert werden. Genauere Informationen findet man in [8].

Der abfragende Computer sendet ein ICMP-Paket des Typs *Echo Request* an den abzufragenden Computer. Dieser antwortet mit *Echo Reply*. Aufgrund dieser Antwort können mindestens zwei Rückschlüsse gezogen werden.

---

[7]Sofern dieses Gerät nicht parallel mit einem zweiten Switch verbunden ist.
[8]Spezifiziert in RFC 792[8]
[9]Vgl. nach RFC792[8], S. 1
[10]Darstellung nach RFC 792

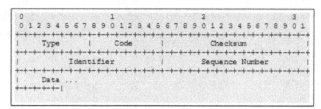

Abbildung 2.4: Telegrammaufbau ICMP[10]

- beide Computer sind miteinander verbunden in einem Netzwerk und

- der Ziel-Computer „lebt".

Diese letzte Information wird häufig dazu genutzt, um eine Aussage über die Funktionsfähigkeit eines Computers zu treffen. Dies ist jedoch nicht immer der Fall.

Bsp.: der Computer ist mittels ICMP erreichbar. Der zu nutzende Dienst wurde jedoch beendet. Aus diesem Grunde müssen weitere Merkmale zur Verifikation, der Funktionsfähigkeit eines Computers herangezogen werden.

2.3.2 DNS - Domain Name System

Der Dienst DNS macht das heutige Internet erst möglich. Computer im Netzwerk haben IP-Adressen mit denen sie angesprochen werden. Diese Adressen, von heute 32 Bit[11], sind für Menschen nur schwer zu merken. Menschen fällt es leichter sich mnemonische Begriffe oder Namen zu merken. Zu diesem Zwecke gibt es das DNS [12]. Der Dienst DNS löst Namen in IP-Adressen auf (auch Hostname Resolution genannt).

Sofern der abzufragende Name sich nicht im Cache[13] des DNS-Server befindet, leitet dieser die Anfrage an seinen übergeordneten DNS weiter. Der Name wird dann über die Top-Level-Domain bis hin zum Computernamen aufgelöst. Die Root-DNS-Server geben Auskunft über die Zuständigkeit der einzelnen Top-Level-Domains. Für Deutschland ist die DeNIC für die Vergabe der DE-Domains zuständig. Danach erfolgt die Zuordnung beim DNS der entsprechenden Domain. Dieser ist verantwortlich für alle Namen in seiner Zone. Die Zone selbst kann in einzelne Subzonen aufgeteilt werden, welche von einem eigenständigen DNS verwaltet werden.

---

[11]Standard IPv4; zukünftig IPv6 hat 128 Bit für den Adressraum
[12]Entwickelt von Paul Mockapetris und definiert in RFC 1033-1035
[13]Als Cache wird ein flüchtiger Zwischenspeicher bezeichnet.

2.3.3 SNMP - Simple Network Management Protocol

SNMP, das Simple Network Management Protocol, dient zur Überwachung und Verwaltung von Netzwerkgeräten. Router, Switche und Hosts lassen sich mit einem Managementtool verwalten. SNMP setzt auf UDP auf und gehört daher zu den verbindungslosen und performanten Protokollen. Im praktischen Einsatz benötigt SNMP weitere Komponenten [14]:

- Mindestens ein Netzelement, welches sich per SNMP fern verwalten lässt. Dieses wird als Agent bezeichnet.

- Ein Manager, der die Agenten verwaltet.

- Eine gemeinsame Datenbasis zum gegenseitigen verstehen von Manager und Agent. Die sogenannte Management Information Base, kurz MIB.

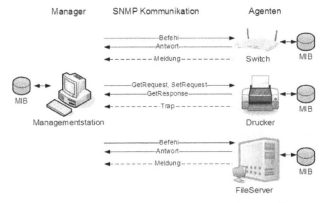

Abbildung 2.5: Kommunikationsmodell für SNMP [15]

Wie in Abbildung 2.5 zu sehen, sendet der Manager Befehle an den Agent. Daraufhin antwortet der Agent mit einer einzelnen Antwort oder einem Satz von Antworten, beispielsweise wenn der Manager nach den verfügbaren Schnittstellen eines Switch gefragt hat. Der Agent hat weiterhin die Möglichkeit den Manager mit einem so genannten Trap, z.B. bei Eintritt eines Ereignisses, zu benachrichtigen. Als solches Ereignis ist beispielsweise die Überschreitung eines Grenzwertes oder der Ausfall einer Komponente zu werten.

Als Grundlage für die Anfragen des Managers und der Antworten der Agenten gilt die MIB. In dieser Datenbank stehen die (Objekt-) Eigenschaften, auf die der

---

[14]Vgl. Barth[2], S. 232f
[15]In Anlehnung an Mitnacht[7], S. 43 und Schwartzkopff[10], S. 1

Agent abgefragt werden kann. Der Aufbau der Datenbank ist hierarchisch und jede Gliederungsstufe wird mit einem Punkt getrennt. Die abzufragenden Objekteingenschaften werden mittels einer OID adressiert. Nachfolgend eine OID für die Eigenschaft Temperatur einer USV: *1.3.6.1.2.1.33.1.2.7.0*

Die Version 3 ist die zur Zeit die Aktuellste der Protokollspezifikation[16]. Die älteren Versionen 1 und 2 sind noch in vielen Geräten implementiert, zu denen Version 3 im wesentlichen abwärtskompatibel ist[17]. SNMPv1 zeichnet sich dadurch aus, dass es nur zwei Zugangskennwörter beherrscht. Eines mit Leserechten und das andere mit Lese- und Schreibrechten. Diese Zugangskennwörter werden auch Community genannt und werden im Klartext im Netz übertragen[18]. In SNMPv3 wurde diese Schwäche durch das „User-based Security Model" und das „View-based Control Model"[19] verbessert.

Ausführliche Beschreibungen sind in den einzelnen RFC festgehalten.

- Version 1 RFCs 1155 bis 1157

- Version 2 1441 bis 1452 und 1901 bis 1910

- Version 3 RFC 3410 bis 3418

- MIB RFC 1213

2.4 Literaturkritik

Die Online-Hilfe [20] zu Nagios von Ethan Galstad ist für den Einstieg ausreichend. Ausführlichere Details kann man dem Buch *Nagios: System- und Netzwerk Monitoring* von Wolfgang Barth[2] entnehmen. Die aktuelle Auflage aus 2008 erklärt zusätzlich zu der Auflage aus 2006[1] die Unterschiede in den Versionen 2 und 3 von Nagios. Auf Erweiterungen für das WebFrontend wird nur minimal eingegangen. Zu dem Abschnitt SNMP werden die Grundlagen soweit vermittelt, dass es möglich ist einige Abfragen durchzuführen. Für tiefer gehende Informationen wird auf weitere Quellen verwiesen.

---

[16]Definiert in RFC 3410-3418
[17]Vgl. Barth[2], S. 237
[18]Vgl. Barth[2], S. 237
[19]Siehe auch RFC3414[3] und RFC3415[12]
[20]URL: http://nagios.sourceforge.net/docs/3_0/

3 Nagios

3.1 Installation

Die (Test-)Installation gliedert sich in zwei Abschnitte. Zum einen werden die Rahmenbedingungen für das Betriebssystem dargestellt und zum anderen wird Nagios selbst installiert.

3.1.1 Betriebssystem

Die Installation erfolgt auf einem Linux-System der Distribution Debian. Verwendet wird die Version 4.03 ETCH mit Kernel 2.6.18 in der Standardversion in einer virtuellen Umgebung. Die virtuelle Umgebung wird mittels VmWare realisiert und ermöglicht die vorhandene Hardware für mehrere unterschiedliche Systeme zu nutzen.

Auf dem Linux-System wird der Webserver Apache2 installiert. Weitere Pakete die zur Installation von Nagios erforderlich sind, sind die libgd-Bibliothek[1] und ein C-Compiler. Beides lässt sich installieren durch den Aufruf

```
#>apt-get install libgd2-dev build-essential
```

Des Weiteren wird für den späteren externen Zugriff ein SSH-Server installiert und die Weiterleitung von Mails an externe Mailserver konfiguriert. Die Konfiguration des eingesetzten Mailservers Exim4 erfolgt mit *dbkg-reconfigure exim4-config* als Smarthost ohne Verteilung.

3.1.2 Nagios-Quellen

Die Installation von Nagios erfolgt aus den Quellen. Hierzu wird ein Download-Verzeichnis erstellt, in dem die Quellen abgelegt werden.

---

[1]Hier findet die Version 2.0.33 Anwendung.

```
#>mkdir ~/downloads
#>wget http://kent[..]/nagios/nagios −3.0.1.tar.gz
#>wget http://kent[..]/nagiosplug/nagios−plugins −1.4.11.tar.gz
```

Nach dem entpacken der beiden Dateien mit *tar xzf* werden aus Gründen der Sicherheit eigene Benutzer und Gruppen für Nagios angelegt.

```
#>useradd nagios −d /usr/local/nagios
#>passwd nagios
#>groupadd nagios
#>usermod −G nagios nagios
#>groupadd nagcmd
#>usermod −G nagcmd nagios
#>usermod −G nagcmd www-data
```

Der nachfolgende Befehl erzeugt nun aus den Quellen die einzelnen Programmteile.

./configure –with-command-group=nagcmd

Nach fertiger Kompilierung werden die Programmteile installiert[2].

```
#>make all
#>make install
#>make install−init
#>make install−config
#>make install−commandmode
#>make install−webconf
```

Der Befehl *make all* übersetzt alle relevanten Programmteile, die *make install* zusammen mit der Dokumentation in die entsprechenden Verzeichnisse kopiert. Mit *make install-init* wird ein Startskript erstellt. Um Nagios nun automatisch starten zu lassen kann man manuell einen symbolischen Link in den passenden RunLevel erstellen oder dies dem Skript *update-rd.d* überlassen. Der Parameter *install-commandmode* bewirkt, dass ein Verzeichnis angelegt wird, in dem später Kommando-Dateien abgelegt werden. Eine Beispielkonfiguration erhält man mit *make install-config*. Der letzte Befehl *make install-webconf* dient der Vorbeitung des WebInterfaces im Apache Webserver.

Die Plugins werden analog kompiliert und installiert.

---

[2]Die einzelnen Schritte der Installation werden in der Nagios Dokumentation von Ethan Galstad[5] ab Seite 325 dargestellt.

```
#>./configure —with-nagios-user=nagios —with-nagios-group=
    nagios
#>make
#>make install
```

Um auf das WebInterface mit Benutzernamen und Kennwort zugreifen zu können, muss noch ein Benutzer definiert werden. Dieser Benutzer kann sich nicht am Betriebssystem direkt anmelden. Der folgende Befehl erzeugt eine neue Datei mit Benutzernamen und verschlüsselten Kennwort:

```
#>htpasswd —c /usr/local/nagios/etc/htpasswd.users nagiosadmin
```

3.2 Konfiguration

Der Pfad der Nagios-Installation ist */usr/local/nagios* [3]. Die Installation bringt bereits eine Beispiel-Konfiguration mit. Diese gilt es nun den eigenen Anforderungen anzupassen. Zur Dokumentation sind die Inhalte der wichtigsten Konfigurationsdateien im Anhang aufgeführt.

nagios.cfg	Hauptkonfigurationsdatei für Nagios laut Init-Skript
command.cfg	Definition Kommandos zur Prüfung
contacts.cfg	Definition der Benachrichtungskontakten
timeperiod.cfg	Definition der Zeitfenster für Prüfung und Benachrichtigung
template.cfg	Definiton mehrere Vorlagen
resource.cfg	Definiton einiger Variablen
infra.cfg	Zusammenfassung aller Geräte nach Klassifizierung Infrastruktur
linux.cfg	Zusammenfassung aller Linux-Geräte
windows.cfg	Zusammenfassung aller Windows-Geräte
hostgroups.cfg	Zusammenfassung der Geräte nach Gruppen
services.cfg	Definition der Dienste für jedes Gerät oder Gruppe

Tabelle 3.1: Überblick der verwendeten Konfigurationsdateien

Da die Netzwerküberwachung sich später über mehrere Standorte verzweigt, wird dies in der nachfolgenden Verzeichnisstruktur bereits berücksichtigt.

```
/usr/local/nagios/etc#.
|-- global
|    |-- commands
|    |-- contacts
```

---

[3]Durch setzen eines symbolischen Links auf */etc/nagios* wird die allgemeine Linux-Verzeichnis-Konvention verbessert

```
|    |-- templates
|    `-- timeperiods
`-- sites
     |-- location1
     |-- location2
     |-- location3
     |    |-- hosts
     |    `-- services
     |-- location4
     |-- location5
     `-- location6
```

Durch Änderung der *nagios.cfg* an der Position von *cfg_dir* können alle Konfigurationsdateien rekursiv zum Stammverzeichnis */usr/local/nagios/etc* eingelesen werden, ohne jede einzelne explizit angeben zu müssen. Des Weiteren wird hier auch das Datumformat entsprechend ISO8601 auf europäisch umgestellt.

3.2.1 System

Jedes Gerät wird aufgeteilt in drei Kategorien, welche die spätere Wartung erleichtern sollen. Diese Kategorien sind Infrastruktur, Linux und Windows. In Abhängigkeit der jeweiligen Kategorie wird das Gerät in einer Konfigurationsdatei als Objekt abgelegt. Beispiel in der Datei *windows.cfg*.

```
define host{
        host_name               DNS01
        alias                   DNS Server
        address                 10.4.1.1
        check_command           check-host-alive
        max_check_attempts      3
        check_period            24x7
        contact_groups          admins
        notification_interval   120
        notification_period     24x7
        notification_options    d,u
        parents                 SWITCHA}
```

Da jeder Server mindestens einen Dienst anbietet, ist es in Nagios verpflichtend mindestens einen Dienst anzugeben. Dies geschieht in der Datei *service.cfg*.

Dienste	ICMP Echo Reply	HTTP GET	DNS Query	MySQL Query	SNMP	TCP/UDP-Port
FIREWALL01	X					
FIREWALL02	X					
SWITCHA	X				X	
SWITCHB	X				X	
WAN01	X					
WAN02	X					
DB01	X			X		
DB02	X			X		
DNS01	X		X			
DNS02	X		X			
WEB01	X	X				
DATA01	X				X	
AE001	X					
AE002	X					
USV01	X				X	
TS00	X					X
TS01	X					X
TS02	X					X

Tabelle 3.2: Geräte-Dienste Übersicht

```
define service{
        service_description     PING
        hostgroup_name          ESN–WIN, ESN–LIN , ESN–INFRA , ESN–TS
        check_command           check_ping!100.0,20%!500.0,60%
        max_check_attempts      3
        normal_check_interval   1
        retry_check_interval    1
        check_period            24x7
        notification_interval   120
        notification_period     workhours
        notification_options    w,u,c,r,f,s
        contact_groups          admins }
```

An dieser Stelle sei erwähnt, dass grundsätzlich die angegebenen Gruppen mittels ICMP Echo Request, Echo Reply geprüft werden. Hier wird als Warnstufe eine Paketlaufzeit von größer 100ms bzw. mehr als 20% Paketverlust definiert. Als kritisch wird die Erreichbarkeit erst betrachtet, wenn die Laufzeit 500ms übersteigt, oder der Paketverlust über 60% liegt.

3.2.2 DNS Server

Die DNS-Server werden anhand ihrer Funktion geprüft. Dies bedeutet, dass eine Abfrage an die DNS-Server gemacht werden und als Resultat eine IP-Adresse erwartet wird. Der passende Service-Eintrag sieht wie folgt aus:

```
define service{
        service_description      DNS-dig
        host_name                DNS01,DNS02
        check_command            check_dig!hostname.domainname
        ...
        }
```

Als Kommando wird hier *check_dns* aufgerufen, welches in der Datei *global/command/command.cfg* definiert ist. Hervorzuheben ist hier, dass der angegebene DNS-Server (Variable *HOSTADDRESS*) nach der IP-Adresse zu den Namen aus der Variablen *ARG1* abgefragt wird.

```
# 'check_dig' command definition
define command{
        command_name    check_dig
        command_line    $USER1$/check_dig -H $HOSTADDRESS$ -1 $
            ARG1$
        }
```

3.2.3 Webserver Intranet

Der Webserver wird ebenfalls anhand seines Dienstes überprüft. Dies geschieht über den Befehl *GET* innerhalb des HTT-Protokoll. Als positive Antwort wird eine HTML-Seite als Ergebnis erwartet mit HTTP Statuscode 200.

```
define service{
        service_description      HTTP
        host_name                WEB01
        check_command            check_http!www.heise.de
        ...
}
```

Die Implementierung in der *command.cfg* nutzt dabei das Kommando *check_http*.

```
# 'check_http' command definition
define command{
        command_name    check_http
```

```
        command_line      $USER1$/check_http -I $HOSTADDRESS$ $
            ARG1$
        }
```

3.2.4 Datenbank Server

Die Datenbank-Server sind installiert mit MySQL 5.0. Die Abfrage auf Funktionsfähigkeit erfolgt durch eine einfachen Connect auf die angegebene Datenbank.

```
define service{
        service_description     MySQL
        host_name               DB01, DB02
        check_command           check_mysql!nagdb
        ...
}
```

Die Implementierung wurde ergänzt durch den Eintrag unten. Das Programm
check_mysql ist eine Erweiterung von NagiosExchange[4], welche eine Sammlung
von zusätzlichen Plugins zur Verfügung stellt. Die Plugins sind im Dateisystem
im Verzeichnis */usr/local/nagios/libexec* untergebracht.

```
# 'check_mysql' command definition
define command{
        command_name        check_mysql
        command_line        $USER1$/check_mysql -H $HOSTADDRESS$ -u
            $USER2$ -p $USER3$ -D $ARG1$
        }
```

Das Plugin nutzt zwei zusätzliche Laufzeitvariablen *USER2* und *USER3*, welche
in der *resource.cfg* definiert sind. In diesem Beispiel haben sie die Belegung von
Benutzernamen und Passwort gegenüber der Datenbank.

3.2.5 Terminalserver

Die Terminalserver haben die Aufgabe, Anwendungen zur Verfügung zu stellen,
welche nicht im lokalen Netz laufen. Aus diesem Grunde befinden sie sich hin-
ter FIREWALL01 und FIREWALL02. Um die Betriebsbereitschaft zu testen, wird
überprüft ob der TCP Port 1494 geöffnet ist.

---

[4]http://www.nagiosexchange.org

```
define service{
        service_description      Citrix
        host_name                TS00 , TS01 , TS02
        check_command            check_citrix
        ...
}
```

Zur Prüfung des offenen Ports macht man sich die Eigenschaft des TC-Protokolls zu Nutze, dass jeder Verbindungsaufbau des Clients durch den Server bestätigt wird. Das Verfahren nennt sich Dreiwege-Handshake[5]. Hierbei wird ausgenutzt, dass bei diesem Verfahren keine Daten übertragen werden und der Betrieb der Terminalserver damit nicht gestört wird.

Es wurde hierfür das vorhandene Programm *check_tcp* verwendet und auf den fixen Port 1494 parametrisiert. Dies ermöglicht einen späteren Austausch des Programms ohne weitere Beeinflussung von anderen Service-Prüfungen die ebenfalls *check_tcp* nutzen.

```
# 'check_citrix' command definition
define command{
        command_name      check_citrix
        command_line      $USER1$/check_tcp –H $HOSTADDRESS$ –p
        1494
}
```

3.2.6 Sonstige

Unterbrechungsfreie Stromversorgung   Die Unterbrechungsfreie Stromversorgung (USV) besitzt einen Ethernet-Port und beherrscht das SNM-Protokoll. Zur Auswertung kommen folgende Grössen:

- Akku-Stand in %

- Quellspannungsverlust

- Bypass

- Temperatur

Wie im Kapitel 2.3.3 erläutert, werden einzelne Grössen mittels OID abgefragt. Bei der USV mit dem Web/SNMP-Adapter CS121 ist für die Temperatur die OID

---

[5]Siehe auch Tanebaum[11], S.588f

1.3.6.1.2.1.33.1.2.7.0 abzufragen. Jede weitere Grösse ist entsprechend dem nachfolgenden Listing zu prüfen.

```
# 'check_usvtemp' command definition
define command{
        command_name      check_usvtemp
        command_line      $USER1$/check_snmp -H $HOSTADDRESS$ -C$
        ARG1$ -o1.3.6.1.2.1.33.1.2.7.0 -w$ARG2$ -c$ARG3$
}
```

Aktive Abfragen der SNMP-Daten haben gegenüber den SNMP-Traps den Vorteil, dass eine definiert Meldung erzeugt werden kann. Ein SNMP-Trap kann im
Netzwerk verloren gehen, ohne dass es den Manager erreicht.

WAN Strecken Die Anbindung an die anderen Standorte ist ein wichtiger Fak-
tor für die Leistungsfähigkeit einer Notruf- und Serviceleitstelle. Die Bandbrei-
tenauslastung ist hierbei ein Indiz für den Bedienungskomfort der Anwendung.
Die Modems besitzen nicht die Fähigkeit von SNMP oder ähnlichem zur Aus-
gabe der aktuellen Bandbreitennutzung. Um an diese Daten zu gelangen, macht
man sich die Eigenschaft des vorangeschalteten Switch zu Nutze. Dieser kann je-
den Port einzeln via SNMP abfragen und daraus ein Ereignis generieren, sobald
der Schwellwert überschritten wird.

Meldungsempfang Server Die DV-gestützten Empfangssysteme sind der Kern
der Notruf- und Serviceleitstelle. Abhängig von der jeweiligen VdS-Klasse sind
unterschiedliche Empfangssysteme vorzuhalten, unabhängig von der Anzahl der
Teilnehmer. Die Einbindung in die Überwachung erfolgt nach den oben genannten Einzelpunkten. Als Überwachungsszenario wird SNMP für die abhängigen
Komponenten des Betriebssystem (Festplattenplatz, CPU-Load, etc) eingesetzt.
Ob die Anwendung ordnungsgemäß funktioniert, welche die Entgegennahme
des Anrufs und die Auswertung des Empfangsprotokolls macht, wird durch die
Prüfung offener TCP/IP-Ports festgestellt.

Die verwendeten Empfangssysteme für analoge Empfangsprotokolle (z.B. Telim)
haben die Eigenschaft, den Mitschnitt der audio-technischen Übertragung im
Dateisystem abzulegen ohne diesen nach einem bestimmten Intervall wieder zu
löschen. Wenn in diesem Verzeichnis mehrere tausend Dateien abgelegt sind, hat
dies Auswirkungen auf das Verhalten des Betriebssystems und der Anwendung.
Dies kann bis zum Stillstand führen. Ein Skript überprüft regelmäßig die Anzahl

der Dateien und löscht gegebenenfalls die Älteren nach einer vorherigen Archivierung. Mit Hilfe des Plugins NRPE für Nagios kann man das Skriptverhalten ebenfalls prüfen [6].

Management Server Die Server für das Meldungsmanagement werden nicht direkt überwacht. Da eine Notruf- und Serviceleitstelle 24 Stunden / 365 Tage im Jahr besetzt ist, wird jede Anomalie[7] direkt durch die verantwortlichen Anwender gemeldet.

3.3 Inbetriebsetzung

Die Konfigurationsdateien können im laufenden Prozess von Nagios eingelesen und aktualisiert werden. Gerade bei Änderungen an den Konfigurationsdateien ist es sinnvoll, diese vor der Aktualisierung auf Fehler zu prüfen. Diese Funktion stellt Nagios mit dem Aufruf *nagios -v /etc/nagios/nagios.cfg* zur Verfügung. Nach erfolgreicher Überprüfung können die Daten mittels */etc/init.d/nagios reload* neu eingelesen werden.

Nagios selbst arbeitet nun intern eine Warteschlange [8] ab. Zuerst wird überprüft, ob der jeweilige Host erreichbar ist. Ist dies positiv, so wird jeder konfigurierte Dienst für den jeweiligen Host geprüft.

Sollte es geschehen, dass ein Dienst oder ein Host negativ gemeldet wird, so erfolgen nun weitere Prüfungen, wie in der Konfiguration vorgesehen. In Abbil-

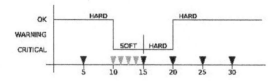

Abbildung 3.1: Zeitlicher Verlauf der Zustandsänderung[9]

dung 3.1 wird der zeitliche Verlauf einer Störung grafisch dargestellt. Im Normalfall prüft Nagios den Dienst hier im Rhythmus von fünf Minuten. In der zehnten

---

[6]Vgl. Jauernig und Lahl[6], S. 25
[7]Unter Anomalie sind schlechte Verbindungszeiten, fehlende Maßnahmen usw. zu verstehen.
[8]engl. Queue
[9]Entnommen von Barth[2], S. 95

Minute tritt ein Fehler auf, welches Nagios veranlasst einen „Soft State" einzulei-
ten. Dieses Ereignis löst noch keine Benachrichtigung aus. Sobald dieser Service,
welcher in einer kürzeren Zeit wiederholt geprüft wird, die maximale Anzahl an
Prüfungen überschritten hat mit weiterhin negativen Ergebnissen, wechselt Nagios in den „Hard State". An dieser Stelle erfolgt der Start der Benachrichtigungs-
kette, wie im Anhang unter B.2 zu sehen. Die weitere Prüfung, ob der Dienst wieder verfügbar ist, erfolgt wieder im normalen Rhythmus. Bei der ersten positven
Prüfung erfolgt wieder ein Wechsel im „Hard State", jedoch als OK.

3.4 WebInterface

Die Bedienung über das WebFrontend erfolgt intuitiv. Die taktische Übersicht[10]
vermittelt einen ersten Blick über die Lage. Auftretende Störungen werden in
mehrere Stufen unterschieden:

1. Netzwerkknoten nicht erreichbar

2. Dienst nicht verfügbar

3. Host nicht erreichbar

Des Weiteren können die konfigurierten Netzwerkteilnehmer in einer übersicht-
licheren Form dargestellt werden. Nagios bietet dazu mehrere vordefinierte An-
sichten. Eine Baumstruktur, wie in Abbildung B.4, erleichtert den Überblick und
zeigt direkt die Abhängigkeiten zu den einzelnen Switchen.

Die Erweiterung NagVis erlaubt es Grafiken mit Piktogrammen zu versehen, welche den aktuellen Status wiedergeben. So lässt sich auf einer Karte von Deutschland auf den ersten Blick erkennen, ob die Strecken und die jeweiligen Standorte
funktionsfähig sind. Eine Ebene tiefer sind die einzelnen Technik-Bereiche ver-
treten sowie die räumliche Anordnung im Rechenzentrum.

3.5 Ausblick

Durch die stetige Erweiterung im Netzwerk sind Anpassungen weiterhin not-
wendig. Die restliche IT-Landschaft wird nun Zug um Zug mit in die Überwachung aufgenommen. Um dem Sicherheitsgedanken der Notruf- und Serviceleitstelle Rechnung zu tragen, wird das System redundant ausgelegt. Dieses übernimmt im Störfall des primären Nagios-Server die weitere Überwachung und

---

[10]Siehe Abbildung im Anhang B.6

Benachrichtigung. Um dabei den Netzwerkverkehr gering zu halten, wird an jedem Standort ein eigenes Netzwerkmanagementsystem installiert, welches dem primären Server über den aktuellen Zustand am Standort eine Nachricht übermittelt. Sollte diese Benachrichtigung ausfallen, wird der primäre Nagios-Server selbst aktiv und prüft die Anbindung, bevor die Administratoren zwecks Behebung der Störung benachrichtigt werden.

4 Fazit

Das Netzwerkmanagementsystem Nagios ist dank seiner modularen Aufbauweise leicht erweiterbar. Jegliche Abfragemöglichkeiten können eingebaut werden durch Perl-Skripte, Plugins oder eigene Programme. Die Berücksichtigung
von Abhängigkeiten der Topologie (Switch-Kaskadierung) erleichtert den Administratoren die Fehleranalyse erheblich. Bei regelmäßigen Audits, zum Beispiel
durch den VdS sowie bei Kundenbesuchen, können die Verfügbarkeitskennzif-
fern nachvollziehbar als Vertriebsinstrument eingesetzt werden bzw. zum Anlass
genommen werden, weitere Massnahmen zu ergreifen. Nagios besitzt eine große
Community, welche bei Problemen schnell und ausführlich hilft. Dies ist viel-
leicht ein Grund warum sich Nagios seit 1999 bis heute erfolgreich hält.

Ein Netzwerkmanagementsystem ist in großen Rechnerlandschaften nicht mehr
wegzudenken. Gerade die Hochverfügbarkeit ist dabei ein besonderer Aspekt.
Im Hinblick einer Notruf- und Serviceleitstelle mit mehreren Standorten ist eine
Überwachung von den angebunden Standorten erforderlich um den Betrieb gut
performant aufrecht zu erhalten.

In dieser Arbeit konnten nur Teilaspekte von Nagios behandelt werden. Weitere Funktionalitäten, wie ein Fail-Over-Monitoring oder die Kaskadierung von
Standorten sind aufgrund ihres Ausmasses nur oberflächlich erwähnt worden.
Die Erkenntnis aus dieser Arbeit ist, dass die Abbildung einer kompletten Notruf-
und Serviceleitstelle in Konfigurationsdateien, ein schwieriges und aufwändiges
Unterfangen ist. Abhängigkeiten zu berücksichtigen und die Alarmempfangsein-
richtung auf die richtigen Ports zu prüfen stellen dabei eine besondere Heraus-
forderung.

Literaturverzeichnis

[1] BARTH, Wolfgang: *Nagios: System and Network Monitoring*. U.S. Ed. No Starch Press, 5 2006. – ISBN: 1593270704

[2] BARTH, Wolfgang: *Nagios: System- und Netzwerk-Monitoring*. 2. Auflage. Open Source Press, 2 2008. – 736 S. – ISBN: 3937514465

[3] BLUMENTHAL, U. ; WIJNEN, B.: Userbased Security Model (USM) for version 3 of the Simple Network Management Protocol (SNMPv3). In: *Network Working Group* (2002), Dezember. – URL http://www.ietf.org/rfc/rfc3414. txt. – Zugriffsdatum: 09.05.2008

[4] BSI: Hinweise zur räumlichen Entfernung zwischen redundanten Rechenzentren / Bundesamt für Sicherheit in der Informationstechnik. URL http://www.bsi.bund.de/gshb/deutsch/hilfmi/doku/RZ-Abstand.pdf. – Zugriffsdatum: 28.04.2008, Mai 2006. – Forschungsbericht

[5] GALSTAD, Ethan: *Nagios Version 3.x Documentation*, Maerz 2007. – URL http://nagios.sourceforge.net/docs/nagios-3.pdf. – Zugriffsdatum: 09.05.2008

[6] JAUERNIG, Matthias ; LAHL, Michael: *Nagios - Grundlegende Einführung und Überwachung von Windows-Rechnern*, Hochschule für Technik, Wirtschaft und Kultur Leipzig, Projektarbeit, Januar 2007. – URL http://www.linux-related.de/studium/nsm/%5BJauernig,Lahl%5D%20Nagios-Ausarbeitung.pdf. – Zugriffsdatum: 06.05.2008

[7] MITNACHT, Sebastian: *Netzwerkmonitoring in einer dynamischen Umgebung*, Universität Koblenz - Landau, Diplomarbeit, September 2006. – URL http://kola.opus.hbz-nrw.de/volltexte/2006/69/pdf/diplomarbeit.pdf. – Zugriffsdatum: 06.05.2008

[8] POSTEL, J.: Internet Control Message Protocol DARPA Internet Program Protocol Specification. In: *Network Working Group* (1981), September. – URL http://www.ietf.org/rfc/rfc792.txt. – Zugriffsdatum: 09.04.2008

[9] RIEGER, Götz: Netz-Controlletti - Netzwerküberwachung mit Nagios / Heise. URL http://www.heise.de/netze/Netz-Controlletti--/artikel/81238. – Zugriffsdatum: 05.05.2008, November 2006. – Forschungsbericht

[10] SCHWARTZKOPFF, Michael: Der Klassiker der Netzwerkadministration: Simple Network Management Protocol. In: *Linux-Magazin* (2006), Nr. 03, S. 6. – URL http://www.linux-magazin.de/heft_abo/ausgaben/2006/03/fernsicht. – Zugriffsdatum: 09.05.2008

[11] TANENBAUM, Andrew S.: *Computernetzwerke*. 4. Pearson Studium, Juli 2003. – 950 S. – ISBN: 9783827370464

[12] WIJNEN, B. ; PRESUHN, R. ; MCCLOGHRIE, K.: Viewbased Access Control Model (VACM) for the Simple Network Management Protocol (SNMP). In: *Network Working Group* (2002), Dezember. – URL http://www.ietf.org/rfc/rfc3415.txt. – Zugriffsdatum: 09.05.2008

Abbildungsquellenverzeichnis

Glossar

Notation	Description
Antwortzeit	Die Antwortzeit stellt die Zeitspanne zwischen dem Ende einer Eingabe und dem Ende der Ausgabe dar. Damit hat sie entscheidende Wirkung auf die Benutzerakzeptanz eines Systems. Wenn der Nutzer aufgrund eines nicht verfügbaren oder überlasteten Systems spürbar warten muss, wird der Nutzer in seinem Arbeitsablauf behindert und empfindet die Arbeit mit dem System als störend.
Ausfallzeit	Ausfallzeiten setzen sich aus geplanten und ungeplanten Ausfallzeiten zusammen. Geplante Ausfallzeiten werden in der Regel durch routinemäßige Wartungsarbeiten ausgelöst, da es für viele Arbeiten an Hard- und Software notwendig ist, das System herunterzufahren. Sie können in Zeitfenstern bei niedriger Systemauslastung durchgeführt werden um den Regelbetrieb nicht zu stark zu stören. Gravierender wirken sich jedoch ungeplante Ausfälle aus, vor allem wenn sie zu Spitzenbelastungszeiten auftreten.
Hardware Redundanz	Redundanz ist das Vorhandensein von mehr als für die Ausführung der vorgesehenen Aufgaben an sich notwendigen Mittel. Die Ausfallsicherheit redundanter Systeme ergibt sich aus der doppelten Auslegung kritischer Einzelkomponenten. Um einen Ausfall des Gesamtsystems herbeizuführen, müssten beide gleichzeitig ausfallen.

Notation	Description
Spanning Tree	Spanning Tree dient zur Erkennung von Schleifen in einem Netzwerksegment. Eines der beiden Interfaces wird hierzu zur Vermeidung von Schleifen deaktiviert. Fehlt nun das andere Netzwerkinterface aus, so wird automatisch durch Spanning Tree die andere Anbindung wieder aufgebaut.
VdS Klasse A für NSL	NSL der Klasse A verfügen ausschließlich über Alarmempfangseinrichtungen (AE) für bedarfsgesteuerte Verbindungen. Zum Beispiel:

- Wählgerät mit anaolgem Teilnehmeranschluß
- Wählgerät für ISDN B-Kanal-Übertragung (X.75)
- Wählverbindung im X.25-Netz als SVC-Verbindung
- Modem für das GSM-Netz

Notation	Description
VdS Klasse B für NSL	NSL der Klasse B verfügen zusätzlich zu den Alarmempfangseinrichtungen für bedarfsgesteuerte Verbindungen auch Alarmempfangseinrichtungen für Ersatzwege in Form von bedarfsgesteuerter Verbindungen gemäß Richtlinie für Übertragungswege VdS 2471. Der Ersatzweg zwischen dem Übertragungsgerät (ÜG) und der Übertragungszentrale muss über eine seperate Trasse geführt werden. Der Ausfall einer der beiden Übertragungswege muss durch die Notruf- und Serviceleitstelle erkannt werden.

Notation	Description
VdS Klasse C für NSL	NSL der Klasse C müssen mindestens über Alarmempfangseinrichtungen der Klasse A oder B verfügen und dazu zusätzlich Alarmempfangseinrichtungen für stehende Verbindungen haben gemäß VdS 2471. Zum Beispiel:

- Festverbindung analog (Standleitung)

- digitale Festverbindung als Datendirektverbindung DES64

- ISDN-Festverbindung X.31

- Festverbindung im X.25-Datennetz

Die zulässigen Übertragungswege sind in der Richtlinie für konforme Übertragunsgwege in Alarmübertragungsanlagen VdS 2532 aufgeführt.

Verfügbarkeit	Die Wahrscheinlichkeit, ein System zu einem vorgegebenen Zeitpunkt in einem funktionsfähigen Zustand anzutreffen.

A Konfigurationsdateien

A.1 commands.cfg

```
1  ###############################################################################
2  # COMMANDS.CFG - COMMAND DEFINITIONS FOR NAGIOS 3.0.1
3  #
4  # Stand: 07.05.2008
5  #
6  #
7  ###############################################################################
8
9  # 'notify-host-by-email' command definition
10 define command{
11         command_name    notify-host-by-email
12         command_line    /usr/bin/printf "%b" "***** Nagios *****\n\nNotification Type: $NOTIFICATIONTYPE$\nHost: $
                           HOSTNAME$\nState: $HOSTSTATE$\nAddress: $HOSTADDRESS$\nInfo: $HOSTOUTPUT$\n\nDate/Time: $
                           LONGDATETIME$\n.\n" | /usr/bin/mail -s '** $NOTIFICATIONTYPE$ Host Alert: $HOSTNAME$ is $HOSTSTATE$
                           **'' $CONTACTEMAIL$
13         #command_line   /usr/bin/printf "%b" "***** Nagios *****\n\nNotification Type: $NOTIFICATIONTYPE$\nHost: $
                           HOSTNAME$\nState: $HOSTSTATE$\nAddress: $HOSTADDRESS$\nInfo: $HOSTOUTPUT$\n\nDate/Time: $
                           LONGDATETIME$\n.\n" >/var/tmp/mailtest
14
15         }
16
17 # 'notify-service-by-email' command definition
18 define command{
19         command_name    notify-service-by-email
20         command_line    /usr/bin/printf "%b" "***** Nagios *****\n\nNotification Type: $NOTIFICATIONTYPE$\n\
                           nService: $SERVICEDESC$\nHost: $HOSTALIAS$\nAddress: $HOSTADDRESS$\nState: $SERVICESTATE$\n\nDate/
                           Time: $LONGDATETIME$\n\nAdditional Info:\n\n$SERVICEOUTPUT$" | /usr/bin/mail -s "** $
                           NOTIFICATIONTYPE$ Service Alert: $HOSTALIAS$/$SERVICEDESC$ is $SERVICESTATE$ **" $CONTACTEMAIL$
21         }
22
23
24 # This command checks to see if a host is "alive" by pinging it
25 # The check must result in a 100% packet loss or 5 second (5000ms) round trip
26 # average time to produce a critical error.
27 # Note: Five ICMP echo packets are sent (determined by the '-p 5' argument)
28
29 # 'check-host-alive' command definition
30 define command{
31         command_name    check-host-alive
32         command_line    $USER1$/check_ping -H $HOSTADDRESS$ -w 3000.0,80% -c 5000.0,100% -p 5
33         }
34
35 # 'check_local_disk' command definition
36 define command{
37         command_name    check_local_disk
38         command_line    $USER1$/check_disk -w $ARG1$ -c $ARG2$ -p $ARG3$
39         }
40
41 # 'check_local_load' command definition
42 define command{
43         command_name    check_local_load
44         command_line    $USER1$/check_load -w $ARG1$ -c $ARG2$
45         }
46
47 # 'check_local_procs' command definition
48 define command{
49         command_name    check_local_procs
50         command_line    $USER1$/check_procs -w $ARG1$ -c $ARG2$ -s $ARG3$
51         }
```

```
52
53  # 'check_local_users' command definition
54  define command{
55          command_name        check_local_users
56          command_line        $USER1$/check_users -w $ARG1$ -c $ARG2$
57          }
58
59  # 'check_local_swap' command definition
60  define command{
61          command_name        check_local_swap
62          command_line        $USER1$/check_swap -w $ARG1$ -c $ARG2$
63          }
64
65  # 'check_local_mrtgtraf' command definition
66  define command{
67          command_name        check_local_mrtgtraf
68          command_line        $USER1$/check_mrtgtraf -F $ARG1$ -a $ARG2$ -w $ARG3$ -c $ARG4$ -e $ARG5$
69          }
70
71  # 'check_ftp' command definition
72  define command{
73          command_name        check_ftp
74          command_line        $USER1$/check_ftp -H $HOSTADDRESS$ $ARG1$
75          }
76
77
78  # 'check_hpjd' command definition
79  define command{
80          command_name        check_hpjd
81          command_line        $USER1$/check_hpjd -H $HOSTADDRESS$ $ARG1$
82          }
83
84
85  # 'check_snmp' command definition
86  define command{
87          command_name        check_snmp
88          command_line        $USER1$/check_snmp -H $HOSTADDRESS$ $ARG1$
89          }
90
91
92  # 'check_http' command definition
93  define command{
94          command_name        check_http
95          command_line        $USER1$/check_http -I $HOSTADDRESS$ $ARG1$
96          }
97
98
99  # 'check_ssh' command definition
100 define command{
101         command_name        check_ssh
102         command_line        $USER1$/check_ssh $ARG1$ $HOSTADDRESS$
103         }
104
105
106 # 'check_dhcp' command definition
107 define command{
108         command_name        check_dhcp
109         command_line        $USER1$/check_dhcp $ARG1$
110         }
111
112 # 'check_dns' command definition
113 define command{
114         command_name        check_dns
115         command_line        $USER1$/check_dns -H $HOSTADDRESS$ --timeout=20
116         }
117
118 # 'check_dig' command definition
119 define command{
120         command_name        check_dig
121         command_line        $USER1$/check_dig -H $HOSTADDRESS$ -l $ARG1$
122         }
123
124 # 'check_ping' command definition
125 define command{
126 .       command_name        check_ping
127         command_line        $USER1$/check_icmp -H $HOSTADDRESS$ -w $ARG1$ -c $ARG2$ -p 5
128         }
129
130
131 # 'check_pop' command definition
```

```
132  define command{
133          command_name      check_pop
134          command_line      $USER1$/check_pop -H $HOSTADDRESS$ $ARG1$
135          }
136
137
138  # 'check_imap' command definition
139  define command{
140          command_name      check_imap
141          command_line      $USER1$/check_imap -H $HOSTADDRESS$ $ARG1$
142          }
143
144
145  # 'check_smtp' command definition
146  define command{
147          command_name      check_smtp
148          command_line      $USER1$/check_smtp -H $HOSTADDRESS$ $ARG1$
149          }
150
151  # 'check_mysql' command definition
152  define command{
153          command_name      check_mysql
154          command_line      $USER1$/check_mysql.pl -H $HOSTADDRESS$ -u nagios -p nagios
155          }
156
157  # 'check_citrix' command definition
158  define command{
159          command_name      check_citrix
160          command_line      $USER1$/check_tcp -H $HOSTADDRESS$ -p 1494
161          }
162
163  # 'check_tcp' command definition
164  define command{
165          command_name      check_tcp
166          command_line      $USER1$/check_tcp -H $HOSTADDRESS$ -p $ARG1$ $ARG2$
167          }
168
169
170  # 'check_udp' command definition
171  define command{
172          command_name      check_udp
173          command_line      $USER1$/check_udp -H $HOSTADDRESS$ -p $ARG1$ $ARG2$
174          }
175
176
177  # 'check_nt' command definition
178  define command{
179          command_name      check_nt
180          command_line      $USER1$/check_nt -H $HOSTADDRESS$ -p 12489 -v $ARG1$ $ARG2$
181          }
182
183
184  # 'check_winhd' command definition
185  define command{
186          command_name      check_winhd
187          command_line      $USER1$/check_winhd.pl -H $HOSTADDRESS$ -C PUBLIC
188          }
189
190  # 'check_usvtemp' command definition
191  define command{
192          command_name      check_usvtemp
193          command_line      $USER1$/check_snmp -H $HOSTADDRESS$ -C$ARG1$ -o1.3.6.1.2.1.33.1.2.7.0 -w$ARG2$ -c$ARG3$
194          }
195
196  ################################################################################
197  #
198  # SAMPLE PERFORMANCE DATA COMMANDS
199  #
200  # These are sample performance data commands that can be used to send performance
201  # data output to two text files (one for hosts, another for services).  If you
202  # plan on simply writing performance data out to a file , consider using the
203  # host_perfdata_file and service_perfdata_file options in the main config file .
204  #
205  ################################################################################
206
207
208  # 'process-host-perfdata' command definition
209  define command{
210          command_name      process-host-perfdata
211          command_line      /usr/bin/printf "%b" "$LASTHOSTCHECK$\t$HOSTNAME$\t$HOSTSTATE$\t$HOSTATTEMPT$\t$
```

```
              HOSTSTATETYPES\t$HOSTEXECUTIONTIME$\t$HOSTOUTPUT$\t$HOSTPERFDATA$\n" >> /usr/local/nagios/var/host-
              perfdata.out
212       }
213
214
215 # 'process-service-perfdata' command definition
216 define command{
217       command_name       process-service-perfdata
218       command_line       /usr/bin/printf "%b" "$LASTSERVICECHECK$\t$HOSTNAME$\t$SERVICEDESC$\t$SERVICESTATE$\t$
              SERVICEATTEMPT$\t$SERVICESTATETYPE$\t$SERVICEEXECUTIONTIME$\t$SERVICELATENCY$\t$SERVICEOUTPUT$\t$
              SERVICEPERFDATA$\n" >> /usr/local/nagios/var/service-perfdata.out
219       }
```

A.2 contacts.cfg

```
 1 ###############################################################################
 2 # CONTACTS.CFG - SAMPLE CONTACT/CONTACTGROUP DEFINITIONS
 3 #
 4 # Last Modified: 05-31-2007
 5 #
 6 # NOTES: This config file provides you with some example contact and contact
 7 #        group definitions that you can reference in host and service
 8 #        definitions.
 9 #
10 #        You don't need to keep these definitions in a separate file from your
11 #        other object definitions.  This has been done just to make things
12 #        easier to understand.
13 #
14 ###############################################################################
15
16
17
18 ###############################################################################
19 ###############################################################################
20 #
21 # CONTACTS
22 #
23 ###############################################################################
24 ###############################################################################
25
26 # Just one contact defined by default - the Nagios admin (that's you)
27 # This contact definition inherits a lot of default values from the 'generic-contact'
28 # template which is defined elsewhere.
29
30 define contact{
31       contact_name           nagiosadmin              ; Short name of user
32       use                    generic-contact          ; Inherit default values from generic-contact
              template (defined above)
33       alias                  Nagios Admin             ; Full name of user
34       email                  michael.glaess@localhost.de   ;
35       }
36 define contact{
37       contact_name           netadmin                 ; Short name of user
38       use                    generic-contact          ; Inherit default values from generic-contact
              template (defined above)
39       alias                  Network Admin            ; Full name of user
40       email                  michael.glaess@localhost.de   ;
41       }
42
43
44
45 ###############################################################################
46 ###############################################################################
47 #
48 # CONTACT GROUPS
49 #
50 ###############################################################################
51 ###############################################################################
52
53 # We only have one contact in this simple configuration file, so there is
54 # no need to create more than one contact group.
55
56 define contactgroup{
57       contactgroup_name      admins
58       alias                  Nagios Administrators
59       members                nagiosadmin, netadmin
```

```
60        }
```

A.3 templates.cfg

```
 1  ###############################################################################
 2  # TEMPLATES.CFG - SAMPLE OBJECT TEMPLATES
 3  #
 4  # Last Modified: 10-03-2007
 5  #
 6  # NOTES: This config file provides you with some example object definition
 7  #        templates that are refered by other host, service, contact, etc.
 8  #        definitions in other config files.
 9  #
10  #        You don't need to keep these definitions in a separate file from your
11  #        other object definitions.  This has been done just to make things
12  #        easier to understand.
13  #
14  ###############################################################################
15
16
17
18  ###############################################################################
19  ###############################################################################
20  #
21  # CONTACT TEMPLATES
22  #
23  ###############################################################################
24  ###############################################################################
25
26  # Generic contact definition template - This is NOT a real contact, just a template!
27
28  define contact{
29        name                          generic-contact      ; The name of this contact template
30        service_notification_period   24x7                 ; service notifications can be sent anytime
31        host_notification_period      24x7                 ; host notifications can be sent anytime
32        service_notification_options  w,u,c,r,f,s          ; send notifications for all service states,
                    flapping events, and scheduled downtime events
33        host_notification_options     d,u,r,f,s            ; send notifications for all host states, flapping
                    events, and scheduled downtime events
34        service_notification_commands notify-service-by-email ; send service notifications via email
35        host_notification_commands    notify-host-by-email ; send host notifications via email
36        register                      0                    ; DONT REGISTER THIS DEFINITION - ITS NOT A REAL
                    CONTACT, JUST A TEMPLATE!
37        }
38
39
40
41
42  ###############################################################################
43  ###############################################################################
44  #
45  # HOST TEMPLATES
46  #
47  ###############################################################################
48  ###############################################################################
49
50  # Generic host definition template - This is NOT a real host, just a template!
51
52  define host{
53        name                          generic-host   ; The name of this host template
54        notifications_enabled         1              ; Host notifications are enabled
55        event_handler_enabled         1              ; Host event handler is enabled
56        flap_detection_enabled        1              ; Flap detection is enabled
57        failure_prediction_enabled    1              ; Failure prediction is enabled
58        process_perf_data             1              ; Process performance data
59        retain_status_information     1              ; Retain status information across program restarts
60        retain_nonstatus_information  1              ; Retain non-status information across program restarts
61        notification_period           24x7           ; Send host notifications at any time
62        register                      0              ; DONT REGISTER THIS DEFINITION - ITS NOT A REAL HOST,
                    JUST A TEMPLATE!
63        }
64
65
66  # Linux host definition template - This is NOT a real host, just a template!
67
68  define host{
```

```
69      name                    linux-server    ; The name of this host template
70      use                     generic-host    ; This template inherits other values from the generic-
           host template
71      check_period            24x7            ; By default, Linux hosts are checked round the clock
72      check_interval          5               ; Actively check the host every 5 minutes
73      retry_interval          1               ; Schedule host check retries at 1 minute intervals
74      max_check_attempts      10              ; Check each Linux host 10 times (max)
75      check_command           check-host-alive ; Default command to check Linux hosts
76      notification_period     workhours       ; Linux admins hate to be woken up, so we only notify
           during the day
77                                              ; Note that the notification_period variable is being
                                                  overridden from
78                                              ; the value that is inherited from the generic-host
                                                  template!
79      notification_interval   120             ; Resend notifications every 2 hours
80      notification_options    d,u,r           ; Only send notifications for specific host states
81      contact_groups          admins          ; Notifications get sent to the admins by default
82      register                0               ; DONT REGISTER THIS DEFINITION - ITS NOT A REAL HOST,
           JUST A TEMPLATE!
83      }
84
85
86
87  # Windows host definition template - This is NOT a real host, just a template!
88
89  define host{
90      name                    windows-server  ; The name of this host template
91      use                     generic-host    ; Inherit default values from the generic-host template
92      check_period            24x7            ; By default, Windows servers are monitored round the clock
93      check_interval          5               ; Actively check the server every 5 minutes
94      retry_interval          1               ; Schedule host check retries at 1 minute intervals
95      max_check_attempts      10              ; Check each server 10 times (max)
96      check_command           check-host-alive    ; Default command to check if servers are "alive"
97      notification_period     24x7            ; Send notification out at any time - day or night
98      notification_interval   30              ; Resend notifications every 30 minutes
99      notification_options    d,r             ; Only send notifications for specific host states
100     contact_groups          admins          ; Notifications get sent to the admins by default
101     hostgroups              windows-servers ; Host groups that Windows servers should be a member of
102     register                0               ; DONT REGISTER THIS - ITS JUST A TEMPLATE
103     }
104
105
106 # We define a generic printer template that can be used for most printers we monitor
107
108 define host{
109     name                    generic-printer ; The name of this host template
110     use                     generic-host    ; Inherit default values from the generic-host template
111     check_period            24x7            ; By default, printers are monitored round the clock
112     check_interval          5               ; Actively check the printer every 5 minutes
113     retry_interval          1               ; Schedule host check retries at 1 minute intervals
114     max_check_attempts      10              ; Check each printer 10 times (max)
115     check_command           check-host-alive    ; Default command to check if printers are "alive"
116     notification_period     workhours       ; Printers are only used during the workday
117     notification_interval   30              ; Resend notifications every 30 minutes
118     notification_options    d,r             ; Only send notifications for specific host states
119     contact_groups          admins          ; Notifications get sent to the admins by default
120     register                0               ; DONT REGISTER THIS - ITS JUST A TEMPLATE
121     }
122
123
124 # Define a template for switches that we can reuse
125 define host{
126     name                    generic-switch  ; The name of this host template
127     use                     generic-host    ; Inherit default values from the generic-host template
128     check_period            24x7            ; By default, switches are monitored round the clock
129     check_interval          5               ; Switches are checked every 5 minutes
130     retry_interval          1               ; Schedule host check retries at 1 minute intervals
131     max_check_attempts      10              ; Check each switch 10 times (max)
132     check_command           check-host-alive    ; Default command to check if routers are "alive"
133     notification_period     24x7            ; Send notifications at any time
134     notification_interval   30              ; Resend notifications every 30 minutes
135     notification_options    d,r             ; Only send notifications for specific host states
136     contact_groups          admins          ; Notifications get sent to the admins by default
137     register                0               ; DONT REGISTER THIS - ITS JUST A TEMPLATE
138     }
139
140
141
142
143 ##############################################################################
```

```
144  ################################################################################
145  #
146  # SERVICE TEMPLATES
147  #
148  ################################################################################
149  ################################################################################
150
151  # Generic service definition template - This is NOT a real service, just a template!
152
153  define service{
154      name                          generic-service        ; The 'name' of this service template
155      active_checks_enabled         1                      ; Active service checks are enabled
156      passive_checks_enabled        1                      ; Passive service checks are enabled/accepted
157      parallelize_check             1                      ; Active service checks should be parallelized (
                 disabling this can lead to major performance problems)
158      obsess_over_service           1                      ; We should obsess over this service (if necessary
                 )
159      check_freshness               0                      ; Default is to NOT check service 'freshness'
160      notifications_enabled         1                      ; Service notifications are enabled
161      event_handler_enabled         1                      ; Service event handler is enabled
162      flap_detection_enabled        1                      ; Flap detection is enabled
163      failure_prediction_enabled    1                      ; Failure prediction is enabled
164      process_perf_data             1                      ; Process performance data
165      retain_status_information     1                      ; Retain status information across program
                 restarts
166      retain_nonstatus_information  1                      ; Retain non-status information across program
                 restarts
167      is_volatile                   0                      ; The service is not volatile
168      check_period                  24x7                   ; The service can be checked at any time of the
                 day
169      max_check_attempts            3                      ; Re-check the service up to 3 times in order to
                 determine its final (hard) state
170      normal_check_interval         10                     ; Check the service every 10 minutes under normal
                 conditions
171      retry_check_interval          2                      ; Re-check the service every two minutes until a
                 hard state can be determined
172      contact_groups                admins                 ; Notifications get sent out to everyone in the '
                 admins' group
173      notification_options          w,u,c,r                ; Send notifications about warning, unknown,
                 critical, and recovery events
174      notification_interval         60                     ; Re-notify about service problems every hour
175      notification_period           24x7                   ; Notifications can be sent out at any time
176      register                      0                      ; DONT REGISTER THIS DEFINITION - ITS NOT A REAL
                 SERVICE, JUST A TEMPLATE!
177      }
178
179
180  # Local service definition template - This is NOT a real service, just a template!
181
182  define service{
183      name                          local-service          ; The name of this service template
184      use                           generic-service        ; Inherit default values from the generic-service
                 definition
185      max_check_attempts            4                      ; Re-check the service up to 4 times in order to
                 determine its final (hard) state
186      normal_check_interval         5                      ; Check the service every 5 minutes under normal
                 conditions
187      retry_check_interval          1                      ; Re-check the service every minute until a hard
                 state can be determined
188      register                      0                      ; DONT REGISTER THIS DEFINITION - ITS NOT A REAL
                 SERVICE, JUST A TEMPLATE!
189      }
```

A.4 timeperiods.cfg

```
1   ################################################################################
2   ################################################################################
3   #
4   # TIME PERIODS
5   #
6   ################################################################################
7   ################################################################################
8
9   # This defines a timeperiod where all times are valid for checks,
10  # notifications , etc. The classic "24x7" support nightmare. :-)
11  define timeperiod{
```

```
12          timeperiod_name 24x7
13          alias                24 Hours A Day, 7 Days A Week
14          sunday               00:00-24:00
15          monday               00:00-24:00
16          tuesday              00:00-24:00
17          wednesday            00:00-24:00
18          thursday             00:00-24:00
19          friday               00:00-24:00
20          saturday             00:00-24:00
21          }
22
23
24  # 'workhours' timeperiod definition
25  define timeperiod{
26          timeperiod_name workhours
27          alias                Normale Dt. Arbeitszeit
28          monday               07:00-17:00
29          tuesday      07:00-17:00
30          wednesday            07:00-17:00
31          thursday             07:00-17:00
32          friday               07:00-14:00
33          }
34
35
36  # 'none' timeperiod definition
37  define timeperiod{
38          timeperiod_name none
39          alias                No Time Is A Good Time
40          }
41
42
43
44  # Note: The timeranges for each holiday are meant to *exclude* the holidays from being
45  # treated as a valid time for notifications, etc. You probably don't want your pager
46  # going off on New Year's. Although you're employer might... :-)
47  define timeperiod{
48          name                 DE-Feiertage
49          timeperiod_name      DE-Feiertage
50          alias                Deutsche Feiertage
51          january 1            00:00-00:00   ; Neujahr
52          may 1                   00:00-00:00   ; Tag der Arbeit
53          october 3            00:00-00:00   ; Tag der Deutschen Einheit
54          december 25          00:00-00:00   ; Weihnachten
55          december 26          00:00-00:00   ; Weihnachten
56          december 31          00:00-00:00   ; Sylvester
57          }
```

A.5 infra.cfg

```
1  #########################################################
2  # Konfigurationsdatei für alle Infrastruktur-Rechner   #
3  # am Standort NSLDE \ ESN                              #
4  #                                                      #
5  # Stand: 07.05.2008                                    #
6  #########################################################
7
8  define host{
9          host_name            FIREWALL01
10         alias                Firewall MS ISA
11         address              10.4.1.254
12         check_command        check-host-alive
13         max_check_attempts   3
14         check_period         24x7
15         contact_groups       admins
16         notification_interval 120
17         notification_period  24x7
18         notification_options d,u
19         parents              SWITCHA
20         icon_image      base/firewall01.png
21         statusmap_image base/firewall01.png
22  }
23
24  define host{
25         host_name            GWSEFW
26         alias                GW Firewall 01
27         address              10.6.199.1
```

```
28          check_command              check-host-alive
29          max_check_attempts         3
30          check_period               24x7
31          contact_groups      admins
32          notification_interval 120
33          notification_period        none
34          notification_options       d,u
35          parents             FIREWALL01,FIREWALL02
36          icon_image                 base/router.png
37          statusmap_image     base/router.png
38  }
39
40  define host{
41          host_name           FIREWALL02
42          alias               Firewall IpTables
43          address             10.4.1.252
44          check_command       check-host-alive
45          max_check_attempts  3
46          check_period        24x7
47          contact_groups      admins
48          notification_interval 120
49          notification_period 24x7
50          notification_options d,u
51          parents             SWITCHB
52          icon_image      base/firewall01.png
53          statusmap_image base/firewall01.png
54  }
55
56  define host{
57          host_name           SWITCHA
58          alias               Core-Switch
59          address             10.4.0.50
60          check_command       check-host-alive
61          max_check_attempts  3
62          check_period        24x7
63          contact_groups      admins
64          notification_interval 120
65          notification_period 24x7
66          notification_options d,u
67          icon_image              base/switch.png
68          statusmap_image base/switch.png
69  }
70
71  define host{
72          host_name           SWITCHB
73          alias               Core-Switch
74          address             10.4.0.51
75          check_command       check-host-alive
76          max_check_attempts  3
77          check_period        24x7
78          contact_groups      admins
79          notification_interval 120
80          notification_period 24x7
81          notification_options d,u
82          icon_image              base/switch.png
83          statusmap_image base/switch.png
84  }
85
86  define host{
87          host_name           SWITCHC
88          alias               Core-Switch
89          address             10.4.0.52
90          check_command       check-host-alive
91          max_check_attempts  3
92          check_period        24x7
93          contact_groups      admins
94          parents             SWITCHA,SWITCHB
95          notification_interval 120
96          notification_period 24x7
97          notification_options d,u
98          icon_image              base/switch.png
99          statusmap_image base/switch.png
100 }
101
102
103 define host{
104         host_name           WAN01
105         alias               WAN Strecke ESN-LOC01
106         address             10.4.0.1
107         check_command       check-host-alive
```

```
108        max_check_attempts      3
109        check_period            24x7
110        contact_groups          admins
111        notification_interval   120
112        notification_period     24x7
113        notification_options    d,u
114        parents                 SWITCHA
115        icon_image              base/linux40.png
116        statusmap_image  base/linux40.png
117 }
118
119 define host{
120        host_name               WAN02
121        alias                   WAN Strecke ESN-LOC02
122        address                 10.4.0.2
123        check_command           check-host-alive
124        max_check_attempts      3
125        check_period            24x7
126        contact_groups          admins
127        notification_interval   120
128        notification_period     24x7
129        notification_options    d,u
130        parents                 SWITCHB
131        icon_image              base/linux40.png
132        statusmap_image  base/linux40.png
133 }
134
135 define host{
136        host_name               USV01
137        alias                   USV Essen
138        address                 10.4.0.100
139        check_command           check-host-alive
140        max_check_attempts      3
141        check_period            24x7
142        contact_groups          admins
143        notification_interval   120
144        notification_period     24x7
145        notification_options    d,u
146        parents                 SWITCHB
147        icon_image              base/linux40.png
148        statusmap_image         base/linux40.png
149 }
```

A.6 linux.cfg

```
1  ##########################################################
2  # Konfigurationsdatei für alle Linux-Rechner            #
3  # am Standort NSLDE \ ESN                                #
4  #                                                        #
5  # Stand: 07.05.2008                                      #
6  ##########################################################
7
8  define host{
9         host_name               DB01
10        alias                   Linux Datenbank Server
11        address                 10.4.1.15
12        check_command           check-host-alive
13        max_check_attempts      3
14        check_period            24x7
15        contact_groups          admins
16        notification_interval   120
17        notification_period     24x7
18        notification_options    d,u
19        parents                 SWITCHA
20        icon_image              base/linux40.png
21        statusmap_image  base/linux40.png
22 }
23
24 define host{
25        host_name               DB02
26        alias                   Linux Datenbank Server
27        address                 10.4.1.16
28        check_command           check-host-alive
29        max_check_attempts      3
30        check_period            24x7
31        contact_groups          admins
```

```
32          notification_interval    120
33          notification_period      24x7
34          notification_options     d,u
35          parents                  SWITCHC
36          icon_image               base/linux40.png
37          statusmap_image base/linux40.png
38   }
```

A.7 windows.cfg

```
1    ##########################################################
2    # Konfigurationsdatei für alle Windows-Rechner        #
3    # am Standort NSLDE \ ESN                             #
4    #                                                     #
5    # Stand: 07.05.2008                                   #
6    ##########################################################
7
8    define host{
9           host_name                DNS01
10          alias                    DNS Server
11          address                  10.4.1.1
12          check_command            check-host-alive
13          max_check_attempts       3
14          check_period             24x7
15          contact_groups           admins
16          notification_interval    120
17          notification_period      24x7
18          notification_options     d,u
19          parents                  SWITCHA
20          icon_image               base/win40.png
21          statusmap_image base/win40.png
22   }
23
24   define host{
25          host_name                DNS02
26          alias                    DNS Server
27          address                  10.4.1.2
28          check_command            check-host-alive
29          max_check_attempts       3
30          check_period             24x7
31          contact_groups           admins
32          notification_interval    120
33          notification_period      24x7
34          notification_options     d,u
35          parents                  SWITCHB
36          icon_image               base/win40.png
37          statusmap_image base/win40.png
38   }
39
40   define host{
41          host_name                WEB01
42          alias                    Web Server
43          address                  10.4.1.5
44          check_command            check-host-alive
45          max_check_attempts       3
46          check_period             24x7
47          contact_groups           admins
48          notification_interval    120
49          notification_period      24x7
50          notification_options     d,u
51          parents                  SWITCHA
52          icon_image               base/win40.png
53          statusmap_image base/win40.png
54   }
55
56   define host{
57          host_name                DATA01
58          alias                    File Server
59          address                  10.4.1.4
60          check_command            check-host-alive
61          max_check_attempts       3
62          check_period             24x7
63          contact_groups           admins
64          notification_interval    120
65          notification_period      24x7
66          notification_options     d,u
```

```
67              parents              SWITCHA
68              icon_image           base/win40.png
69              statusmap_image base/win40.png
70    }
71
72    define host{
73              host_name            AE4001
74              alias                Telefonie Server
75              address              10.4.1.21
76              check_command        check-host-alive
77              max_check_attempts   3
78              check_period         24x7
79              contact_groups       admins
80              notification_interval  120
81              notification_period  24x7
82              notification_options d,u
83              parents              SWITCHA
84              icon_image           base/win40.png
85              statusmap_image base/win40.png
86    }
87
88    define host{
89              host_name            AE4002
90              alias                Telefonie Server
91              address              10.4.1.22
92              check_command        check-host-alive
93              max_check_attempts   3
94              check_period         24x7
95              contact_groups       admins
96              notification_interval  120
97              notification_period  24x7
98              notification_options d,u
99              parents              SWITCHA
100             icon_image           base/win40.png
101             statusmap_image base/win40.png
102   }
103   define host{
104             host_name            TS00
105             alias                TS ESN
106             address              ts00.local.net
107             check_command        check-host-alive
108             max_check_attempts   3
109             check_period         24x7
110             contact_groups       admins
111             notification_interval  120
112             notification_period  24x7
113             notification_options d,u
114             parents              FIREWALL01
115             icon_image           base/citrix_7.png
116             statusmap_image base/citrix_7.png
117   }
118   define host{
119             host_name            TS01
120             alias                TS ESN
121             address              ts01.local.net
122             check_command        check-host-alive
123             max_check_attempts   3
124             check_period         24x7
125             contact_groups       admins
126             notification_interval  120
127             notification_period  24x7
128             notification_options d,u
129             parents              FIREWALL01
130             icon_image           base/citrix_7.png
131             statusmap_image base/citrix_7.png
132   }
133   define host{
134             host_name            TS02
135             alias                TS ESN
136             address              ts02.local.net
137             check_command        check-host-alive
138             max_check_attempts   3
139             check_period         24x7
140             contact_groups       admins
141             notification_interval  120
142             notification_period  24x7
143             notification_options d,u
144             parents              FIREWALL01
145             icon_image           base/citrix_7.png
146             statusmap_image base/citrix_7.png
```

```
147  }
```

A.8 hostgroups.cfg

```
1  ##########################################################
2  # Konfigurationsdatei für alle Gruppe            #
3  # am Standort NSLDE \ ESN                        #
4  #                                                #
5  # Stand: 07.05.2008                              #
6  ##########################################################
7
8  define hostgroup{
9          hostgroup_name    NSLDE-ESN
10         alias                                       NSL Standort Essen
11         hostgroup_members  ESN-WIN, ESN-LIN , ESN-INFRA , ESN-TS
12  }
13
14  define hostgroup{
15         hostgroup_name    ESN-WIN
16         alias                                       Windows Server ESN
17         hostgroup_members         ESN-DNS, ESN-TEL , ESN-WEB, ESN-FILE
18  }
19
20  define hostgroup{
21         hostgroup_name    ESN-LIN
22         alias                                       Linux Server ESN
23         hostgroup_members         ESN-DB
24  }
25
26  define hostgroup{
27         hostgroup_name    ESN-INFRA
28         alias                                       Infra Server ESN
29         hostgroup_members         ESN-WAN, ESN-FW, ESN-SWITCH
30         members            GWSEFW, SEUSV01
31  }
32
33  define hostgroup{
34         hostgroup_name    ESN-DNS
35         alias                                       DNS Server ESN
36         members                           DNS01, DNS02
37  }
38
39  define hostgroup{
40         hostgroup_name    ESN-DB
41         alias                                       DB Server ESN
42         members                           DB01, DB02
43  }
44
45  define hostgroup{
46         hostgroup_name    ESN-TEL
47         alias                                       Telefonie Server ESN
48         members                           AE4001 , AE4002
49  }
50
51  define hostgroup{
52         hostgroup_name    ESN-WEB
53         alias                                       WEB Server ESN
54         members                           WEB01
55  }
56
57  define hostgroup{
58         hostgroup_name    ESN-FILE
59         alias                                       File Server ESN
60         members                           DATA01
61  }
62
63  define hostgroup{
64         hostgroup_name    ESN-WAN
65         alias                                       WAN Strecken ESN
66         members                           WAN01, WAN02
67  }
68
69  define hostgroup{
70         hostgroup_name    ESN-SWITCH
71         alias                                       Switch ESN
72         members                           SWITCHA, SWITCHB, SWITCHC
```

```
73  }
74
75  define hostgroup {
76          hostgroup_name    ESN-FW
77          alias                                     Firewall ESN
78          members                          FIREWALL01, FIREWALL02
79  }
80  define hostgroup {
81          hostgroup_name    ESN-TS
82          alias                                     Terminalserver ESN
83          members                          TS00, TS01, TS02
84  }
```

A.9 services.cfg

```
1   ########################################################
2   # Konfigurationsdatei für alle Services            #
3   # am Standort NSLDE \ ESN                          #
4   #                                                  #
5   # Stand: 07.05.2008                                #
6   ########################################################
7
8   define service {
9           service_description              PING
10          hostgroup_name           ESN-WIN, ESN-LIN, ESN-INFRA, ESN-TS
11          check_command                    check_ping!100.0,25%!500.0,60%
12          max_check_attempts               3
13          normal_check_interval    1
14          retry_check_interval             1
15          check_period                     24x7
16          notification_interval    120
17          notification_period              workhours
18          notification_options             w,u,c,r,f,s
19          contact_groups           admins
20  }
21
22  define service {
23          service_description              DNS-dig
24          host_name                        DNS01, DNS02
25          check_command                    check_dig!www.google.de
26          max_check_attempts               3
27          normal_check_interval    1
28          retry_check_interval             1
29          check_period                     24x7
30          notification_interval    120
31          notification_period              none
32          notification_options             w,u,c,r,f,s
33          contact_groups           admins
34  }
35
36  define service {
37          service_description              HTTP
38          host_name                        WEB01
39          check_command                    check_http!www.heise.de
40          max_check_attempts               3
41          normal_check_interval    1
42          retry_check_interval             1
43          check_period                     24x7
44          notification_interval    120
45          notification_period              none
46          notification_options             w,u,c,r,f,s
47          contact_groups           admins
48  }
49  define service {
50          service_description              MySQL
51          host_name                        DB01, DB02
52          check_command                    check_mysql
53          max_check_attempts               3
54          normal_check_interval            1
55          retry_check_interval             1
56          check_period                     24x7
57          notification_interval    120
58          notification_period              none
59          notification_options             w,u,c,r,f,s
60          contact_groups           admins
61  }
```

```
62  define service{
63          service_description                      Citrix
64          host_name                                TS00 , TS01 , TS02
65          check_command                            check_citrix
66          max_check_attempts                       3
67          normal_check_interval        1
68          retry_check_interval                     1
69          check_period                             24x7
70          notification_interval        120
71          notification_period                      none
72          notification_options                     w,u,c,r,f,s
73          contact_groups               admins
74  }
75
76  define service{
77          service_description                      USV-Temp
78          host_name                                USV01
79          check_command                            check_usvtemp ! public !25!30
80          max_check_attempts                       3
81          normal_check_interval                    1
82          retry_check_interval                     1
83          check_period                             24x7
84          notification_interval                    120
85          notification_period                      24x7
86          notification_options                     w,u,c,r,f,s
87          contact_groups                           admins
88  }
```

A.10 nagios.cfg

```
1   ###############################################################################
2   #
3   # NAGIOS.CFG - Main Config File for Nagios 3.0.1
4   #
5   #
6   # Stand: 07.05.2008
7   #
8   ###############################################################################
9
10
11  # LOG FILE
12  log_file=/usr/local/nagios/var/nagios.log
13
14  # OBJECT CONFIGURATION FILE(S)
15  # These are the object configuration files in which you define hosts ,
16  # host groups, contacts , contact groups, services , etc.
17  # You can split your object definitions across several config files
18  # if you wish (as shown below), or keep them all in a single config file.
19
20  # You can also tell Nagios to process all config files (with a .cfg
21  # extension) in a particular directory by using the cfg_dir
22  # directive as shown below:
23  cfg_dir=/usr/local/nagios/etc/global
24  cfg_dir=/usr/local/nagios/etc/nslde
25
26  # OBJECT CACHE FILE
27  object_cache_file=/usr/local/nagios/var/objects.cache
28
29  # PRE-CACHED OBJECT FILE
30  precached_object_file=/usr/local/nagios/var/objects.precache
31
32  # RESOURCE FILE
33  resource_file=/usr/local/nagios/etc/resource.cfg
34
35  # STATUS FILE
36  status_file=/usr/local/nagios/var/status.dat
37
38  # STATUS FILE UPDATE INTERVAL
39  status_update_interval=10
40
41  # NAGIOS USER
42  nagios_user=nagios
43
44  # NAGIOS GROUP
45  nagios_group=nagios
46
```

```
47  # EXTERNAL COMMAND OPTION
48  check_external_commands=1
49
50  # EXTERNAL COMMAND CHECK INTERVAL
51  command_check_interval=-1
52
53  # EXTERNAL COMMAND FILE
54  command_file=/usr/local/nagios/var/rw/nagios.cmd
55
56  # EXTERNAL COMMAND BUFFER SLOTS
57  external_command_buffer_slots=4096
58
59  # LOCK FILE
60  lock_file=/usr/local/nagios/var/nagios.lock
61
62  # TEMP FILE
63  temp_file=/usr/local/nagios/var/nagios.tmp
64
65  # TEMP PATH
66  temp_path=/tmp
67
68  # EVENT BROKER OPTIONS
69  # Controls what (if any) data gets sent to the event broker.
70  # Values:  0     = Broker nothing
71  #         -1     = Broker everything
72  #         <other> = See documentation
73
74  event_broker_options=102913
75  #-1
76
77  # EVENT BROKER MODULE(S)
78  # This directive is used to specify an event broker module that should
79  # by loaded by Nagios at startup.  Use multiple directives if you want
80  # to load more than one module.  Arguments that should be passed to
81  # the module at startup are seperated from the module path by a space.
82  #
83  #!!!!!!!!!!!!!!!!!!!!!!!!!!!!!!!!!!!!!!!!!!!!!!!!!!!!!!!!!!!!!!!!!!!!!!!!
84  # WARNING !!! WARNING !!! WARNING !!! WARNING !!! WARNING !!! WARNING
85  #!!!!!!!!!!!!!!!!!!!!!!!!!!!!!!!!!!!!!!!!!!!!!!!!!!!!!!!!!!!!!!!!!!!!!!!!
86  #
87  # Do NOT overwrite modules while they are being used by Nagios or Nagios
88  # will crash in a fiery display of SEGFAULT glory.  This is a bug/limitation
89  # either in dlopen(), the kernel, and/or the filesystem.  And maybe Nagios...
90  #
91  # The correct/safe way of updating a module is by using one of these methods:
92  #    1. Shutdown Nagios, replace the module file, restart Nagios
93  #    2. Delete the original module file, move the new module file into place, restart Nagios
94  #
95  # Example:
96  #
97  #    broker_module=<modulepath> [moduleargs]
98
99  #broker_module=/somewhere/module1.o
100 #broker_module=/somewhere/module2.o arg1 arg2=3 debug=0
101
102 # LOG ROTATION METHOD
103 # This is the log rotation method that Nagios should use to rotate
104 # the main log file.  Values are as follows..
105 #    n     = None - don't rotate the log
106 #    h     = Hourly rotation (top of the hour)
107 #    d     = Daily rotation (midnight every day)
108 #    w     = Weekly rotation (midnight on Saturday evening)
109 #    m     = Monthly rotation (midnight last day of month)
110
111 log_rotation_method=d
112
113 # LOG ARCHIVE PATH
114 # This is the directory where archived (rotated) log files should be
115 # placed (assuming you've chosen to do log rotation).
116
117 log_archive_path=/usr/local/nagios/var/archives
118
119 # LOGGING OPTIONS
120 # If you want messages logged to the syslog facility, as well as the
121 # Nagios log file set this option to 1.  If not, set it to 0.
122
123 use_syslog=1
124
125 # NOTIFICATION LOGGING OPTION
126 # If you don't want notifications to be logged, set this value to 0.
```

```
127  # If notifications should be logged, set the value to 1.
128
129  log_notifications=1
130
131  # SERVICE RETRY LOGGING OPTION
132  # If you don't want service check retries to be logged, set this value
133  # to 0.  If retries should be logged, set the value to 1.
134
135  log_service_retries=1
136
137  # HOST RETRY LOGGING OPTION
138  # If you don't want host check retries to be logged, set this value to
139  # 0.  If retries should be logged, set the value to 1.
140
141  log_host_retries=1
142
143  # EVENT HANDLER LOGGING OPTION
144  # If you don't want host and service event handlers to be logged, set
145  # this value to 0.  If event handlers should be logged, set the value
146  # to 1.
147
148  log_event_handlers=1
149
150  # INITIAL STATES LOGGING OPTION
151  # If you want Nagios to log all initial host and service states to
152  # the main log file (the first time the service or host is checked)
153  # you can enable this option by setting this value to 1.  If you
154  # are not using an external application that does long term state
155  # statistics reporting, you do not need to enable this option.  In
156  # this case, set the value to 0.
157
158  log_initial_states=0
159
160  # EXTERNAL COMMANDS LOGGING OPTION
161  # If you don't want Nagios to log external commands, set this value
162  # to 0.  If external commands should be logged, set this value to 1.
163  # Note: This option does not include logging of passive service
164  # checks - see the option below for controlling whether or not
165  # passive checks are logged.
166
167  log_external_commands=1
168
169  # PASSIVE CHECKS LOGGING OPTION
170  # If you don't want Nagios to log passive host and service checks, set
171  # this value to 0.  If passive checks should be logged, set
172  # this value to 1.
173
174  log_passive_checks=1
175
176  # GLOBAL HOST AND SERVICE EVENT HANDLERS
177  # These options allow you to specify a host and service event handler
178  # command that is to be run for every host or service state change.
179  # The global event handler is executed immediately prior to the event
180  # handler that you have optionally specified in each host or
181  # service definition. The command argument is the short name of a
182  # command definition that you define in your host configuration file.
183  # Read the HTML docs for more information.
184
185  #global_host_event_handler=somecommand
186  #global_service_event_handler=somecommand
187
188  # SERVICE INTER-CHECK DELAY METHOD
189  # This is the method that Nagios should use when initially
190  # "spreading out" service checks when it starts monitoring.  The
191  # default is to use smart delay calculation, which will try to
192  # space all service checks out evenly to minimize CPU load.
193  # Using the dumb setting will cause all checks to be scheduled
194  # at the same time (with no delay between them)!  This is not a
195  # good thing for production, but is useful when testing the
196  # parallelization functionality.
197  #      n       = None - don't use any delay between checks
198  #      d       = Use a "dumb" delay of 1 second between checks
199  #      s       = Use "smart" inter-check delay calculation
200  #      x.xx    = Use an inter-check delay of x.xx seconds
201
202  service_inter_check_delay_method=s
203
204  # MAXIMUM SERVICE CHECK SPREAD
205  # This variable determines the timeframe (in minutes) from the
206  # program start time that an initial check of all services should
```

```
207  # be completed.  Default is 30 minutes.
208
209  max_service_check_spread=30
210
211  # SERVICE CHECK INTERLEAVE FACTOR
212  # This variable determines how service checks are interleaved.
213  # Interleaving the service checks allows for a more even
214  # distribution of service checks and reduced load on remote
215  # hosts.  Setting this value to 1 is equivalent to how versions
216  # of Nagios previous to 0.0.5 did service checks.  Set this
217  # value to s (smart) for automatic calculation of the interleave
218  # factor unless you have a specific reason to change it.
219  #        s        = Use "smart" interleave factor calculation
220  #        x        = Use an interleave factor of x, where x is a
221  #                   number greater than or equal to 1.
222
223  service_interleave_factor=s
224
225  # HOST INTER-CHECK DELAY METHOD
226  # This is the method that Nagios should use when initially
227  # "spreading out" host checks when it starts monitoring.  The
228  # default is to use smart delay calculation, which will try to
229  # space all host checks out evenly to minimize CPU load.
230  # Using the dumb setting will cause all checks to be scheduled
231  # at the same time (with no delay between them)!
232  #        n        = None - don't use any delay between checks
233  #        d        = Use a "dumb" delay of 1 second between checks
234  #        s        = Use "smart" inter-check delay calculation
235  #        x.xx     = Use an inter-check delay of x.xx seconds
236
237  host_inter_check_delay_method=s
238
239  # MAXIMUM HOST CHECK SPREAD
240  # This variable determines the timeframe (in minutes) from the
241  # program start time that an initial check of all hosts should
242  # be completed.  Default is 30 minutes.
243
244  max_host_check_spread=30
245
246  # MAXIMUM CONCURRENT SERVICE CHECKS
247  # This option allows you to specify the maximum number of
248  # service checks that can be run in parallel at any given time.
249  # Specifying a value of 1 for this variable essentially prevents
250  # any service checks from being parallelized.  A value of 0
251  # will not restrict the number of concurrent checks that are
252  # being executed.
253
254  max_concurrent_checks=0
255
256  # HOST AND SERVICE CHECK REAPER FREQUENCY
257  # This is the frequency (in seconds!) that Nagios will process
258  # the results of host and service checks.
259
260  check_result_reaper_frequency=10
261
262  # MAX CHECK RESULT REAPER TIME
263  # This is the max amount of time (in seconds) that  a single
264  # check result reaper event will be allowed to run before
265  # returning control back to Nagios so it can perform other
266  # duties.
267
268  max_check_result_reaper_time=30
269
270  # CHECK RESULT PATH
271  # This is directory where Nagios stores the results of host and
272  # service checks that have not yet been processed.
273  #
274  # Note: Make sure that only one instance of Nagios has access
275  # to this directory!
276
277  check_result_path=/usr/local/nagios/var/spool/checkresults
278
279  # MAX CHECK RESULT FILE AGE
280  # This option determines the maximum age (in seconds) which check
281  # result files are considered to be valid.  Files older than this
282  # threshold will be mercilessly deleted without further processing.
283
284  max_check_result_file_age=3600
285
286  # CACHED HOST CHECK HORIZON
```

```
287  # This option determines the maximum amount of time (in seconds)
288  # that the state of a previous host check is considered current.
289  # Cached host states (from host checks that were performed more
290  # recently that the timeframe specified by this value) can immensely
291  # improve performance in regards to the host check logic.
292  # Too high of a value for this option may result in inaccurate host
293  # states being used by Nagios, while a lower value may result in a
294  # performance hit for host checks.  Use a value of 0 to disable host
295  # check caching.
296
297  cached_host_check_horizon=15
298
299  # CACHED SERVICE CHECK HORIZON
300  # This option determines the maximum amount of time (in seconds)
301  # that the state of a previous service check is considered current.
302  # Cached service states (from service checks that were performed more
303  # recently that the timeframe specified by this value) can immensely
304  # improve performance in regards to predictive dependency checks.
305  # Use a value of 0 to disable service check caching.
306
307  cached_service_check_horizon=15
308
309  # ENABLE PREDICTIVE HOST DEPENDENCY CHECKS
310  # This option determines whether or not Nagios will attempt to execute
311  # checks of hosts when it predicts that future dependency logic test
312  # may be needed.  These predictive checks can help ensure that your
313  # host dependency logic works well.
314  # Values:
315  #  0 = Disable predictive checks
316  #  1 = Enable predictive checks (default)
317
318  enable_predictive_host_dependency_checks=1
319
320  # ENABLE PREDICTIVE SERVICE DEPENDENCY CHECKS
321  # This option determines whether or not Nagios will attempt to execute
322  # checks of service when it predicts that future dependency logic test
323  # may be needed.  These predictive checks can help ensure that your
324  # service dependency logic works well.
325  # Values:
326  #  0 = Disable predictive checks
327  #  1 = Enable predictive checks (default)
328
329  enable_predictive_service_dependency_checks=1
330
331  # SOFT STATE DEPENDENCIES
332  # This option determines whether or not Nagios will use soft state
333  # information when checking host and service dependencies. Normally
334  # Nagios will only use the latest hard host or service state when
335  # checking dependencies. If you want it to use the latest state (regardless
336  # of whether its a soft or hard state type), enable this option.
337  # Values:
338  #  0 = Don't use soft state dependencies (default)
339  #  1 = Use soft state dependencies
340
341  soft_state_dependencies=0
342
343  # AUTO-RESCHEDULING OPTION
344  # This option determines whether or not Nagios will attempt to
345  # automatically reschedule active host and service checks to
346  # "smooth" them out over time.  This can help balance the load on
347  # the monitoring server.
348  # WARNING: THIS IS AN EXPERIMENTAL FEATURE - IT CAN DEGRADE
349  # PERFORMANCE, RATHER THAN INCREASE IT, IF USED IMPROPERLY
350
351  auto_reschedule_checks=0
352
353  # AUTO-RESCHEDULING INTERVAL
354  # This option determines how often (in seconds) Nagios will
355  # attempt to automatically reschedule checks.  This option only
356  # has an effect if the auto_reschedule_checks option is enabled.
357  # Default is 30 seconds.
358  # WARNING: THIS IS AN EXPERIMENTAL FEATURE - IT CAN DEGRADE
359  # PERFORMANCE, RATHER THAN INCREASE IT, IF USED IMPROPERLY
360
361  auto_rescheduling_interval=30
362
363  # AUTO-RESCHEDULING WINDOW
364  # This option determines the "window" of time (in seconds) that
365  # Nagios will look at when automatically rescheduling checks.
366  # Only host and service checks that occur in the next X seconds
```

```
367  # (determined by this variable) will be rescheduled. This option
368  # only has an effect if the auto_reschedule_checks option is
369  # enabled.  Default is 180 seconds (3 minutes).
370  # WARNING: THIS IS AN EXPERIMENTAL FEATURE - IT CAN DEGRADE
371  # PERFORMANCE, RATHER THAN INCREASE IT, IF USED IMPROPERLY
372
373  auto_rescheduling_window=180
374
375  # SLEEP TIME
376  # This is the number of seconds to sleep between checking for system
377  # events and service checks that need to be run.
378
379  sleep_time=0.25
380
381  # TIMEOUT VALUES
382  # These options control how much time Nagios will allow various
383  # types of commands to execute before killing them off.  Options
384  # are available for controlling maximum time allotted for
385  # service checks, host checks, event handlers, notifications, the
386  # ocsp command, and performance data commands.  All values are in
387  # seconds.
388
389  service_check_timeout=60
390  host_check_timeout=30
391  event_handler_timeout=30
392  notification_timeout=30
393  ocsp_timeout=5
394  perfdata_timeout=5
395
396  # RETAIN STATE INFORMATION
397  # This setting determines whether or not Nagios will save state
398  # information for services and hosts before it shuts down.  Upon
399  # startup Nagios will reload all saved service and host state
400  # information before starting to monitor.  This is useful for
401  # maintaining long-term data on state statistics, etc, but will
402  # slow Nagios down a bit when it (re)starts.  Since its only
403  # a one-time penalty, I think its well worth the additional
404  # startup delay.
405
406  retain_state_information=1
407
408  # STATE RETENTION FILE
409  # This is the file that Nagios should use to store host and
410  # service state information before it shuts down.  The state
411  # information in this file is also read immediately prior to
412  # starting to monitor the network when Nagios is restarted.
413  # This file is used only if the preserve_state_information
414  # variable is set to 1.
415
416  state_retention_file=/usr/local/nagios/var/retention.dat
417
418  # RETENTION DATA UPDATE INTERVAL
419  # This setting determines how often (in minutes) that Nagios
420  # will automatically save retention data during normal operation.
421  # If you set this value to 0, Nagios will not save retention
422  # data at regular interval, but it will still save retention
423  # data before shutting down or restarting.  If you have disabled
424  # state retention, this option has no effect.
425
426  retention_update_interval=60
427
428  # USE RETAINED PROGRAM STATE
429  # This setting determines whether or not Nagios will set
430  # program status variables based on the values saved in the
431  # retention file.  If you want to use retained program status
432  # information, set this value to 1.  If not, set this value
433  # to 0.
434
435  use_retained_program_state=1
436
437  # USE RETAINED SCHEDULING INFO
438  # This setting determines whether or not Nagios will retain
439  # the scheduling info (next check time) for hosts and services
440  # based on the values saved in the retention file.  If you
441  # If you want to use retained scheduling info, set this
442  # value to 1.  If not, set this value to 0.
443
444  use_retained_scheduling_info=1
445
446  # RETAINED ATTRIBUTE MASKS (ADVANCED FEATURE)
```

```
447  # The following variables are used to specify specific host and
448  # service attributes that should *not* be retained by Nagios during
449  # program restarts.
450  #
451  # The values of the masks are bitwise ANDs of values specified
452  # by the "MODATTR_" definitions found in include/common.h.
453  # For example, if you do not want the current enabled/disabled state
454  # of flap detection and event handlers for hosts to be retained, you
455  # would use a value of 24 for the host attribute mask...
456  # MODATTR_EVENT_HANDLER_ENABLED (8) + MODATTR_FLAP_DETECTION_ENABLED (16) = 24
457
458  # This mask determines what host attributes are not retained
459  retained_host_attribute_mask=0
460
461  # This mask determines what service attributes are not retained
462  retained_service_attribute_mask=0
463
464  # These two masks determine what process attributes are not retained.
465  # There are two masks, because some process attributes have host and service
466  # options.  For example, you can disable active host checks, but leave active
467  # service checks enabled.
468  retained_process_host_attribute_mask=0
469  retained_process_service_attribute_mask=0
470
471  # These two masks determine what contact attributes are not retained.
472  # There are two masks, because some contact attributes have host and
473  # service options.  For example, you can disable host notifications for
474  # a contact, but leave service notifications enabled for them.
475  retained_contact_host_attribute_mask=0
476  retained_contact_service_attribute_mask=0
477
478  # INTERVAL LENGTH
479  # This is the seconds per unit interval as used in the
480  # host/contact/service configuration files.  Setting this to 60 means
481  # that each interval is one minute long (60 seconds).  Other settings
482  # have not been tested much, so your mileage is likely to vary...
483
484  interval_length=60
485
486  # AGGRESSIVE HOST CHECKING OPTION
487  # If you don't want to turn on aggressive host checking features, set
488  # this value to 0 (the default).  Otherwise set this value to 1 to
489  # enable the aggressive check option.  Read the docs for more info
490  # on what aggressive host check is or check out the source code in
491  # base/checks.c
492
493  use_aggressive_host_checking=0
494
495  # SERVICE CHECK EXECUTION OPTION
496  # This determines whether or not Nagios will actively execute
497  # service checks when it initially starts.  If this option is
498  # disabled, checks are not actively made, but Nagios can still
499  # receive and process passive check results that come in.  Unless
500  # you're implementing redundant hosts or have a special need for
501  # disabling the execution of service checks, leave this enabled!
502  # Values: 1 = enable checks, 0 = disable checks
503
504  execute_service_checks=1
505
506  # PASSIVE SERVICE CHECK ACCEPTANCE OPTION
507  # This determines whether or not Nagios will accept passive
508  # service checks results when it initially (re)starts.
509  # Values: 1 = accept passive checks, 0 = reject passive checks
510
511  accept_passive_service_checks=1
512
513  # HOST CHECK EXECUTION OPTION
514  # This determines whether or not Nagios will actively execute
515  # host checks when it initially starts.  If this option is
516  # disabled, checks are not actively made, but Nagios can still
517  # receive and process passive check results that come in.  Unless
518  # you're implementing redundant hosts or have a special need for
519  # disabling the execution of host checks, leave this enabled!
520  # Values: 1 = enable checks, 0 = disable checks
521
522  execute_host_checks=1
523
524  # PASSIVE HOST CHECK ACCEPTANCE OPTION
525  # This determines whether or not Nagios will accept passive
526  # host checks results when it initially (re)starts.
```

```
527  # Values: 1 = accept passive checks , 0 = reject passive checks
528
529  accept_passive_host_checks=1
530
531  # NOTIFICATIONS OPTION
532  # This determines whether or not Nagios will sent out any host or
533  # service notifications when it is initially (re)started.
534  # Values: 1 = enable notifications , 0 = disable notifications
535
536  enable_notifications=1
537
538  # EVENT HANDLER USE OPTION
539  # This determines whether or not Nagios will run any host or
540  # service event handlers when it is initially (re)started. Unless
541  # you're implementing redundant hosts, leave this option enabled.
542  # Values: 1 = enable event handlers, 0 = disable event handlers
543
544  enable_event_handlers=1
545
546  # PROCESS PERFORMANCE DATA OPTION
547  # This determines whether or not Nagios will process performance
548  # data returned from service and host checks. If this option is
549  # enabled, host performance data will be processed using the
550  # host_perfdata_command (defined below) and service performance
551  # data will be processed using the service_perfdata_command (also
552  # defined below). Read the HTML docs for more information on
553  # performance data.
554  # Values: 1 = process performance data, 0 = do not process performance data
555
556  process_performance_data=0
557
558  # HOST AND SERVICE PERFORMANCE DATA PROCESSING COMMANDS
559  # These commands are run after every host and service check is
560  # performed. These commands are executed only if the
561  # enable_performance_data option (above) is set to 1. The command
562  # argument is the short name of a command definition that you
563  # define in your host configuration file. Read the HTML docs for
564  # more information on performance data.
565
566  #host_perfdata_command=process-host-perfdata
567  #service_perfdata_command=process-service-perfdata
568
569  # HOST AND SERVICE PERFORMANCE DATA FILES
570  # These files are used to store host and service performance data.
571  # Performance data is only written to these files if the
572  # enable_performance_data option (above) is set to 1.
573
574  #host_perfdata_file=/tmp/host-perfdata
575  #service_perfdata_file=/tmp/service-perfdata
576
577  # HOST AND SERVICE PERFORMANCE DATA FILE TEMPLATES
578  # These options determine what data is written (and how) to the
579  # performance data files. The templates may contain macros, special
580  # characters (\t for tab, \r for carriage return, \n for newline)
581  # and plain text. A newline is automatically added after each write
582  # to the performance data file. Some examples of what you can do are
583  # shown below.
584
585  #host_perfdata_file_template=[HOSTPERFDATA]\t$TIMET$\t$HOSTNAME$\t$HOSTEXECUTIONTIME$\t$HOSTOUTPUT$\t$HOSTPERFDATA
       $
586  #service_perfdata_file_template=[SERVICEPERFDATA]\t$TIMET$\t$HOSTNAME$\t$SERVICEDESC$\t$SERVICEEXECUTIONTIME$\t$
       SERVICELATENCY$\t$SERVICEOUTPUT$\t$SERVICEPERFDATA$
587
588  # HOST AND SERVICE PERFORMANCE DATA FILE MODES
589  # This option determines whether or not the host and service
590  # performance data files are opened in write ("w") or append ("a")
591  # mode. If you want to use named pipes, you should use the special
592  # pipe ("p") mode which avoid blocking at startup, otherwise you will
593  # likely want the defult append ("a") mode.
594
595  #host_perfdata_file_mode=a
596  #service_perfdata_file_mode=a
597
598  # HOST AND SERVICE PERFORMANCE DATA FILE PROCESSING INTERVAL
599  # These options determine how often (in seconds) the host and service
600  # performance data files are processed using the commands defined
601  # below. A value of 0 indicates the files should not be periodically
602  # processed.
603
604  #host_perfdata_file_processing_interval=0
```

```
605  #service_perfdata_file_processing_interval=0
606
607  # HOST AND SERVICE PERFORMANCE DATA FILE PROCESSING COMMANDS
608  # These commands are used to periodically process the host and
609  # service performance data files.  The interval at which the
610  # processing occurs is determined by the options above.
611
612  #host_perfdata_file_processing_command=process-host-perfdata-file
613  #service_perfdata_file_processing_command=process-service-perfdata-file
614
615  # OBSESS OVER SERVICE CHECKS OPTION
616  # This determines whether or not Nagios will obsess over service
617  # checks and run the ocsp_command defined below.  Unless you're
618  # planning on implementing distributed monitoring, do not enable
619  # this option.  Read the HTML docs for more information on
620  # implementing distributed monitoring.
621  # Values: 1 = obsess over services, 0 = do not obsess (default)
622
623  obsess_over_services=0
624
625  # OBSESSIVE COMPULSIVE SERVICE PROCESSOR COMMAND
626  # This is the command that is run for every service check that is
627  # processed by Nagios.  This command is executed only if the
628  # obsess_over_services option (above) is set to 1.  The command
629  # argument is the short name of a command definition that you
630  # define in your host configuration file. Read the HTML docs for
631  # more information on implementing distributed monitoring.
632
633  #ocsp_command=somecommand
634
635  # OBSESS OVER HOST CHECKS OPTION
636  # This determines whether or not Nagios will obsess over host
637  # checks and run the ochp_command defined below.  Unless you're
638  # planning on implementing distributed monitoring, do not enable
639  # this option.  Read the HTML docs for more information on
640  # implementing distributed monitoring.
641  # Values: 1 = obsess over hosts, 0 = do not obsess (default)
642
643  obsess_over_hosts=0
644
645  # OBSESSIVE COMPULSIVE HOST PROCESSOR COMMAND
646  # This is the command that is run for every host check that is
647  # processed by Nagios.  This command is executed only if the
648  # obsess_over_hosts option (above) is set to 1.  The command
649  # argument is the short name of a command definition that you
650  # define in your host configuration file. Read the HTML docs for
651  # more information on implementing distributed monitoring.
652
653  #ochp_command=somecommand
654
655  # TRANSLATE PASSIVE HOST CHECKS OPTION
656  # This determines whether or not Nagios will translate
657  # DOWN/UNREACHABLE passive host check results into their proper
658  # state for this instance of Nagios.  This option is useful
659  # if you have distributed or failover monitoring setup.  In
660  # these cases your other Nagios servers probably have a different
661  # "view" of the network, with regards to the parent/child relationship
662  # of hosts.  If a distributed monitoring server thinks a host
663  # is DOWN, it may actually be UNREACHABLE from the point of
664  # this Nagios instance.  Enabling this option will tell Nagios
665  # to translate any DOWN or UNREACHABLE host states it receives
666  # passively into the correct state from the view of this server.
667  # Values: 1 = perform translation, 0 = do not translate (default)
668
669  translate_passive_host_checks=0
670
671  # PASSIVE HOST CHECKS ARE SOFT OPTION
672  # This determines whether or not Nagios will treat passive host
673  # checks as being HARD or SOFT.  By default, a passive host check
674  # result will put a host into a HARD state type.  This can be changed
675  # by enabling this option.
676  # Values: 0 = passive checks are HARD, 1 = passive checks are SOFT
677
678  passive_host_checks_are_soft=0
679
680  # ORPHANED HOST/SERVICE CHECK OPTIONS
681  # These options determine whether or not Nagios will periodically
682  # check for orphaned host service checks.  Since service checks are
683  # not rescheduled until the results of their previous execution
684  # instance are processed, there exists a possibility that some
```

```
685  # checks may never get rescheduled.  A similar situation exists for
686  # host checks, although the exact scheduling details differ a bit
687  # from service checks.  Orphaned checks seem to be a rare
688  # problem and should not happen under normal circumstances.
689  # If you have problems with service checks never getting
690  # rescheduled, make sure you have orphaned service checks enabled.
691  # Values: 1 = enable checks, 0 = disable checks
692
693  check_for_orphaned_services=1
694  check_for_orphaned_hosts=1
695
696
697
698  # SERVICE FRESHNESS CHECK OPTION
699  # This option determines whether or not Nagios will periodically
700  # check the "freshness" of service results.  Enabling this option
701  # is useful for ensuring passive checks are received in a timely
702  # manner.
703  # Values: 1 = enabled freshness checking, 0 = disable freshness checking
704
705  check_service_freshness=1
706
707
708
709  # SERVICE FRESHNESS CHECK INTERVAL
710  # This setting determines how often (in seconds) Nagios will
711  # check the "freshness" of service check results.  If you have
712  # disabled service freshness checking, this option has no effect.
713
714  service_freshness_check_interval=60
715
716
717
718  # HOST FRESHNESS CHECK OPTION
719  # This option determines whether or not Nagios will periodically
720  # check the "freshness" of host results.  Enabling this option
721  # is useful for ensuring passive checks are received in a timely
722  # manner.
723  # Values: 1 = enabled freshness checking, 0 = disable freshness checking
724
725  check_host_freshness=0
726
727
728
729  # HOST FRESHNESS CHECK INTERVAL
730  # This setting determines how often (in seconds) Nagios will
731  # check the "freshness" of host check results.  If you have
732  # disabled host freshness checking, this option has no effect.
733
734  host_freshness_check_interval=60
735
736
737
738
739  # ADDITIONAL FRESHNESS THRESHOLD LATENCY
740  # This setting determines the number of seconds that Nagios
741  # will add to any host and service freshness thresholds that
742  # it calculates (those not explicitly specified by the user).
743
744  additional_freshness_latency=15
745
746
747
748
749  # FLAP DETECTION OPTION
750  # This option determines whether or not Nagios will try
751  # and detect hosts and services that are "flapping".
752  # Flapping occurs when a host or service changes between
753  # states too frequently.  When Nagios detects that a
754  # host or service is flapping, it will temporarily suppress
755  # notifications for that host/service until it stops
756  # flapping.  Flap detection is very experimental, so read
757  # the HTML documentation before enabling this feature!
758  # Values: 1 = enable flap detection
759  #         0 = disable flap detection (default)
760
761  enable_flap_detection=1
762
763
764
```

```
765  # FLAP DETECTION THRESHOLDS FOR HOSTS AND SERVICES
766  # Read the HTML documentation on flap detection for
767  # an explanation of what this option does.  This option
768  # has no effect if flap detection is disabled.
769
770  low_service_flap_threshold=5.0
771  high_service_flap_threshold=20.0
772  low_host_flap_threshold=5.0
773  high_host_flap_threshold=20.0
774
775
776
777  # DATE FORMAT OPTION
778  # This option determines how short dates are displayed. Valid options
779  # include:
780  #      us              (MM-DD-YYYY HH:MM:SS)
781  #      euro            (DD-MM-YYYY HH:MM:SS)
782  #      iso8601         (YYYY-MM-DD HH:MM:SS)
783  #      strict-iso8601  (YYYY-MM-DDTHH:MM:SS)
784  #
785
786  date_format=iso8601
787
788
789
790
791  # TIMEZONE OFFSET
792  # This option is used to override the default timezone that this
793  # instance of Nagios runs in.  If not specified, Nagios will use
794  # the system configured timezone.
795  #
796  # NOTE: In order to display the correct timezone in the CGIs, you
797  # will also need to alter the Apache directives for the CGI path
798  # to include your timezone.  Example:
799  #
800  #    <Directory "/usr/local/nagios/sbin/">
801  #       SetEnv TZ "Australia/Brisbane"
802  #       ...
803  #    </Directory>
804
805  #use_timezone=US/Mountain
806  #use_timezone=Australia/Brisbane
807
808
809
810
811  # P1.PL FILE LOCATION
812  # This value determines where the pl.pl perl script (used by the
813  # embedded Perl interpreter) is located.  If you didn't compile
814  # Nagios with embedded Perl support, this option has no effect.
815
816  p1_file=/usr/local/nagios/bin/p1.pl
817
818
819
820  # EMBEDDED PERL INTERPRETER OPTION
821  # This option determines whether or not the embedded Perl interpreter
822  # will be enabled during runtime.  This option has no effect if Nagios
823  # has not been compiled with support for embedded Perl.
824  # Values: 0 = disable interpreter , 1 = enable interpreter
825
826  enable_embedded_perl=1
827
828
829
830  # EMBEDDED PERL USAGE OPTION
831  # This option determines whether or not Nagios will process Perl plugins
832  # and scripts with the embedded Perl interpreter if the plugins/scripts
833  # do not explicitly indicate whether or not it is okay to do so. Read
834  # the HTML documentation on the embedded Perl interpreter for more
835  # information on how this option works.
836
837  use_embedded_perl_implicitly=1
838
839
840
841  # ILLEGAL OBJECT NAME CHARACTERS
842  # This option allows you to specify illegal characters that cannot
843  # be used in host names, service descriptions , or names of other
844  # object types.
```

```
845
846 illegal_object_name_chars='~!$%^&*|'"<>?,()='
847
848
849
850 # ILLEGAL MACRO OUTPUT CHARACTERS
851 # This option allows you to specify illegal characters that are
852 # stripped from macros before being used in notifications, event
853 # handlers, etc.  This DOES NOT affect macros used in service or
854 # host check commands.
855 # The following macros are stripped of the characters you specify:
856 #       $HOSTOUTPUT$
857 #       $HOSTPERFDATA$
858 #       $HOSTACKAUTHOR$
859 #       $HOSTACKCOMMENT$
860 #       $SERVICEOUTPUT$
861 #       $SERVICEPERFDATA$
862 #       $SERVICEACKAUTHOR$
863 #       $SERVICEACKCOMMENT$
864
865 illegal_macro_output_chars='~$&|'"<>'
866
867
868
869 # REGULAR EXPRESSION MATCHING
870 # This option controls whether or not regular expression matching
871 # takes place in the object config files.  Regular expression
872 # matching is used to match host, hostgroup, service, and service
873 # group names/descriptions in some fields of various object types.
874 # Values: 1 = enable regexp matching, 0 = disable regexp matching
875
876 use_regexp_matching=0
877
878
879
880 # "TRUE" REGULAR EXPRESSION MATCHING
881 # This option controls whether or not "true" regular expression
882 # matching takes place in the object config files.  This option
883 # only has an effect if regular expression matching is enabled
884 # (see above).  If this option is DISABLED, regular expression
885 # matching only occurs if a string contains wildcard characters
886 # (* and ?).  If the option is ENABLED, regexp matching occurs
887 # all the time (which can be annoying).
888 # Values: 1 = enable true matching, 0 = disable true matching
889
890 use_true_regexp_matching=0
891
892
893
894 # ADMINISTRATOR EMAIL/PAGER ADDRESSES
895 # The email and pager address of a global administrator (likely you).
896 # Nagios never uses these values itself, but you can access them by
897 # using the $ADMINEMAIL$ and $ADMINPAGER$ macros in your notification
898 # commands.
899
900 admin_email=nagios@localhost
901 admin_pager=pagenagios@localhost
902
903
904
905 # DAEMON CORE DUMP OPTION
906 # This option determines whether or not Nagios is allowed to create
907 # a core dump when it runs as a daemon.  Note that it is generally
908 # considered bad form to allow this, but it may be useful for
909 # debugging purposes.  Enabling this option doesn't guarantee that
910 # a core file will be produced, but that's just life...
911 # Values: 1 - Allow core dumps
912 #         0 - Do not allow core dumps (default)
913
914 daemon_dumps_core=0
915
916
917
918 # LARGE INSTALLATION TWEAKS OPTION
919 # This option determines whether or not Nagios will take some shortcuts
920 # which can save on memory and CPU usage in large Nagios installations.
921 # Read the documentation for more information on the benefits/tradeoffs
922 # of enabling this option.
923 # Values: 1 - Enabled tweaks
924 #         0 - Disable tweaks (default)
```

```
925
926  use_large_installation_tweaks=0
927
928
929
930  # ENABLE ENVIRONMENT MACROS
931  # This option determines whether or not Nagios will make all standard
932  # macros available as environment variables when host/service checks
933  # and system commands (event handlers, notifications, etc.) are
934  # executed.  Enabling this option can cause performance issues in
935  # large installations, as it will consume a bit more memory and (more
936  # importantly) consume more CPU.
937  # Values: 1 - Enable environment variable macros (default)
938  #         0 - Disable environment variable macros
939
940  enable_environment_macros=1
941
942
943
944  # CHILD PROCESS MEMORY OPTION
945  # This option determines whether or not Nagios will free memory in
946  # child processes (processed used to execute system commands and host/
947  # service checks).  If you specify a value here, it will override
948  # program defaults.
949  # Value: 1 - Free memory in child processes
950  #        0 - Do not free memory in child processes
951
952  #free_child_process_memory=1
953
954
955
956  # CHILD PROCESS FORKING BEHAVIOR
957  # This option determines how Nagios will fork child processes
958  # (used to execute system commands and host/service checks).  Normally
959  # child processes are fork()ed twice, which provides a very high level
960  # of isolation from problems.  Fork()ing once is probably enough and will
961  # save a great deal on CPU usage (in large installs), so you might
962  # want to consider using this.  If you specify a value here, it will
963  # program defaults.
964  # Value: 1 - Child processes fork() twice
965  #        0 - Child processes fork() just once
966
967  #child_processes_fork_twice=1
968
969
970
971  # DEBUG LEVEL
972  # This option determines how much (if any) debugging information will
973  # be written to the debug file.  OR values together to log multiple
974  # types of information.
975  # Values: -1 = Everything
976  #          0 = Nothing
977  #          1 = Functions
978  #          2 = Configuration
979  #          4 = Process information
980  #          8 = Scheduled events
981  #         16 = Host/service checks
982  #         32 = Notifications
983  #         64 = Event broker
984  #        128 = Check IPC
985
986  debug_level=0
987
988
989
990  # DEBUG VERBOSITY
991  # This option determines how verbose the debug log out will be.
992  # Values: 0 = Brief output
993  #         1 = More detailed
994  #         2 = Very detailed
995
996  debug_verbosity=1
997
998
999
1000 # DEBUG FILE
1001 # This option determines where Nagios should write debugging information.
1002
1003 debug_file=/usr/local/nagios/var/nagios.debug
1004
```

```
1005
1006
1007  # MAX DEBUG FILE SIZE
1008  # This option determines the maximum size (in bytes) of the debug file.  If
1009  # the file grows larger than this size, it will be renamed with a .old
1010  # extension.  If a file already exists with a .old extension it will
1011  # automatically be deleted.  This helps ensure your disk space usage doesn't
1012  # get out of control when debugging Nagios.
1013
1014  max_debug_file_size=1000000
```

A.11 resource.cfg

```
 1  ###########################################################################
 2  #
 3  # RESOURCE.CFG - Sample Resource File for Nagios 3.0.1
 4  #
 5  # Last Modified: 09-10-2003
 6  #
 7  # You can define $USERx$ macros in this file, which can in turn be used
 8  # in command definitions in your host config file(s).  $USERx$ macros are
 9  # useful for storing sensitive information such as usernames, passwords,
10  # etc.  They are also handy for specifying the path to plugins and
11  # event handlers - if you decide to move the plugins or event handlers to
12  # a different directory in the future, you can just update one or two
13  # $USERx$ macros, instead of modifying a lot of command definitions.
14  #
15  # The CGIs will not attempt to read the contents of resource files, so
16  # you can set restrictive permissions (600 or 660) on them.
17  #
18  # Nagios supports up to 32 $USERx$ macros ($USER1$ through $USER32$)
19  #
20  # Resource files may also be used to store configuration directives for
21  # external data sources like MySQL...
22  #
23  ###########################################################################

24
25  # Sets $USER1$ to be the path to the plugins
26  $USER1$=/usr/local/nagios/libexec
27
28  # Sets $USER2$ to be the path to event handlers
29  #$USER2$=/usr/local/nagios/libexec/eventhandlers
30
31  # Store some usernames and passwords (hidden from the CGIs)
32  #$USER3$=WEB
33  #$USER4$=WEB
```

B Abbildungen

Nachfolgend einige Abbildungen zur Installation und während des Betriebs.

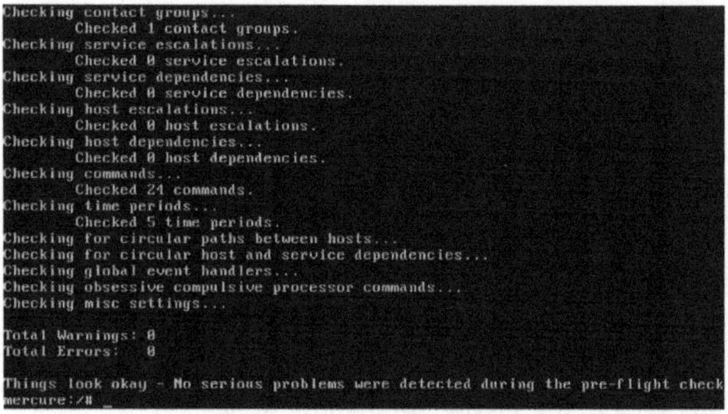

Abbildung B.1: Prüfung der Konfiguration

---

[1]Entnommen von Rieger[9], S. 3

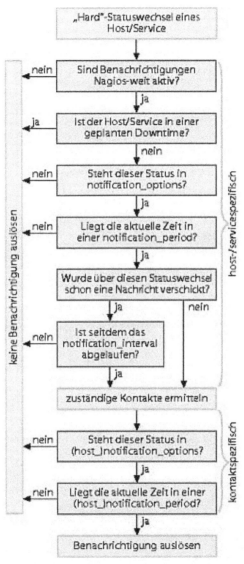

Abbildung B.2: Benachrichtigungsfilter [1]

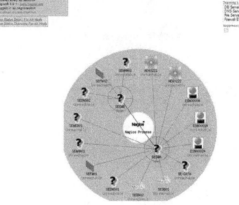

Abbildung B.3: Netzwerkübersicht

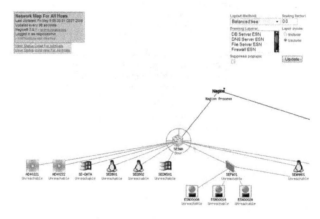

Abbildung B.4: Netzwerkübersicht Baumstruktur

Abbildung B.5: Aktueller Status Nagios Host

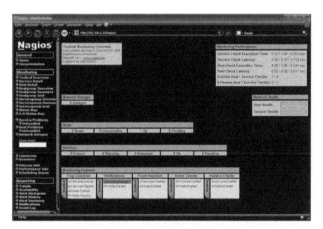

Abbildung B.6: Taktischer Überblick